all about
parenting

PARENTING PLAYBOOK

• 15 minutes a day •

Volume I

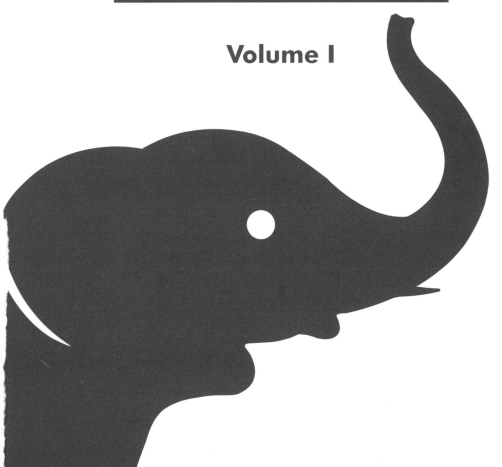

ISBN : 978-1-7377486-0-1

e-mail: hello@allaboutparenting.com
website: allaboutparenting.com

I'm doing All About Parenting for

Stick a photo of your kid(s) here!

Contents

CLOSER TO COOPERATION IN JUST 15 MINUTES A DAY

My promise to _____

When?

Where?

How?

Please read the next 2 pages before coming back to fill in this page.

Your Promise

Welcome to the journey to being the best parent you can be for your child!

The journey may seem long, but you've already taken **the first step – and the most important one**. You're here!

Step 2 is planning:

:: **When? Where? How?**

First of all, choose **when** you'd like to follow the programme, for 15 minutes a day.

Will it be 6.30 am, over coffee before the kids wake up? 8.10 am, before anyone else arrives at the office? During your afternoon break at 3 pm? .

Then, choose **where** you'll be for those 15 minutes alone with the programme.

In an armchair at home? At the kitchen table? In your office?

Lastly, choose **how** you'll set yourself up for the programme.

With a cup of coffee? Or is it tea? Using an old red biro or your favourite fountain pen? With or without headphones?

Step 3

Fill in the details on the previous page.

For example
When? — Between 7 and 7.15 am, before the kids wake up
Where? — At the kitchen table
How? — With a cup of coffee

This is the promise you are making to your child – a consistent and sustained effort and a new routine that you'll make your own. A promise for a better relationship between you and a brighter future for you both.

15 minutes may not be much. But...
Imagine if you were steering a ship across the Atlantic and changing course by just one degree each day. Nobody would notice that shift. But the difference at the end of the voyage could see you either shipwrecked somewhere off the Sahara or sailing serenely into Lisbon.

:: Your child's refusals

The next few pages are a checklist. Use them to write down the objectives that you want to keep in mind as you progress through All About Parenting.

What does the ideal relationship with your child look like? Make a list of the refusals, challenging behaviours and 'problems' you have in your relationship with your child.

As you advance through the programme and apply the techniques, you'll see those problems start to disappear.

Tick the box whenever you see that one of the types of behaviour you described has been dealt with or an objective has been reached. Most of the episodes in the programme end with practical exercises.

:: PQ test

We measure intelligence in IQ points. We measure emotional intelligence in EQ points.

And now, we've created a test whereby you can measure your intelligence as a parent. Head to **AllAboutParenting.co.uk/PQ** and take the test.

Write your results on the PQ page.

:: Exercises

You'll find them here in this Playbook.

The information will sink in with every exercise you do, and make it much more likely you'll actually use the techniques you've learnt in theory.

Basically, you'll cut your learning time in half. The same is true of the time it takes to see improvements in your relationship with your child.

:: Notes

We've left a few blank pages at the end of each chapter for your notes.

Use them to write down the ideas, techniques and questions you want to remember. They'll be useful when you want to go back over certain things.

:: What you've learnt

There's a self-evaluation test at the end of each chapter. See for yourself how well you've taken the information on board and which episodes you might need to watch again.

If you prefer working with pen and paper, fill out the test in your Playbook and check the answers at the back.

And if you're more tech-savvy, scan the QR code and you'll be able to take the test right there on your smartphone.

:: Appendix

The Playbook's appendix includes some extra 'goodies'. We've packed it full of worksheets, posters and techniques that you can photocopy and fill out for each child or whenever you come across a new situation. Every time you see this symbol , it means that you'll find the same exercise in the appendix.

Keep this Playbook close at hand. It is as valuable as the video episodes you'll be following online. The episodes and the Parenting Playbook together form All About Parenting.

With love,
Patrick Ney

PQ Test

> Head to **AllAboutParenting.co.uk/PQ** and see what your parenting quotient is.
>
> Repeat the test after 5 months — halfway through the programme — and again once you've worked your way through all the episodes.

PQ test 1 results: **Date:**

Comments:

PQ test 2 results: **Date:**

Comments:

PQ test 3 results: **Date:**

Comments:

Note to Self

❯ Write a message to the parent you will be in 10 months' time. What do you want to remember? What words of encouragement would you like to hear?

Date:

Your Objectives

❯ Write down your child's refusals, the problems you want to avoid and your objectives.
Tick the box when you consider the problem solved.

1

THE ESSENTIALS OF PARENT-CHILD COOPERATION

Chapter 1 Contents

The Essentials of Parent-Child Cooperation

🕐 10 mins

Why Do Children Say 'No'?

❯ Sort the types of refusals according to the Basic Psychological Need that is not being fulfilled.

Write down the behaviour that each of these 3 Basic Psychological Needs triggers.

Need for Relatedness

The need to love and be loved unconditionally
The need to give and receive
The need to be recognised, respected and valued

Challenging behaviour:

_____

_____

_____

_____

_____

_____

_____

_____

_____

_____

_____

_____

▼ 4%

Need for Competence

The Need to know, learn and develop
The Need to feel capable
Manifests itself positively in the question 'Why?'

Challenging behaviour:

9%

Need for Autonomy

The Need to make their own choices and decisions and be the source of their own actions
'Let me do it by myself!'

Challenging behaviour:

🕐 10 mins

What Kind of Parent Are You?

❯ Think about your parenting style and the parenting styles of the other members of your family. Fill in the table below.

Person	Parenting style	Characteristics

▾ 17%

🕐 8 mins 📖 p. 250

How to Set Rules and Boundaries

❯ Think about the refusals and challenging behaviours you identified in the first episode.
Write down the rules that can help you prevent refusals for each of the following categories.

Rules about bedtime and waking up

_____

_____

_____

_____

_____

_____

Rules about eating

_____

_____

_____

_____

_____

_____

▼ 22%

Rules about hygiene

_____
_____
_____
_____
_____
_____
_____
_____

Rules about housekeeping

_____
_____
_____
_____
_____
_____
_____
_____
_____

▼ 26%

Rules about screens

_____

_____

_____

_____

_____

_____

_____

_____

_____

Rules about personal property

_____

_____

_____

_____

_____

_____

_____

_____

_____

▼ 30%

Episode 9

9 mins

The First 2 Techniques: 'Planning Ahead' and 'Sequencing'

➤ **Put the rules and boundaries that you have already established into words using these techniques.**

PLANNING AHEAD

Always tell your child what is about to happen. 'You've got 20 minutes, then we're getting ready for bed.'

SEQUENCING

Replace 'if' with 'after'.
'Mum, can I go and play with my friends?'
'Of course you can, after you've tidied your toys away.'

35%

🕐 7 mins

The Next 2 Techniques:
'Conditional Yes' and 'Options Within Limits'

❯ Put the rules and boundaries that you have already established into words using these techniques.

YES, IF...

The objective is to avoid the word 'no' as much as possible by using 'yes' with conditions attached. 'Mum, can I watch cartoons?'
'Yes, **if** you agree to turn them off after 10 minutes, because we're getting ready to go out.'

_____

_____

_____

_____

_____

_____

OPTIONS WITHIN LIMITS

Empathy➔   2-3 alternatives within pre-set limits   ➔
        'You choose'/'You decide'/'It's your choice'

'I **understand** that you'd prefer not to brush your teeth right now. You need to have clean teeth when you go to bed. Which toothpaste do you want to use, **this one or that one?** It's your choice.'

_____

_____

_____

_____

_____

▼ 39%

🕐 6 mins

What to Do If It Still Doesn't Work

❯ What are the 2 types of consequences?

_____

_____

❯ What are the conditions that a natural consequence has to fulfil?

_____

_____

❯ Think about the refusals your child has made. What are the natural consequences that you could allow to happen?

Child's refusal	Natural consequence

▼ 43%

4 mins

Find Logical Consequences and Apply Them

❯ What are the conditions that logical consequences have to fulfil?

_____

_____

❯ Choose 2 examples of challenging behaviour and write down the logical consequence you could apply to each one below.
Word it in the way you learnt in today's episode.

> Behaviour:

>Consequence:

> Behaviour:

>Consequence:

▼ 48%

 12 mins

What to Do If Your Kid Refuses to Turn Off Screens

❯ Set a rule on screen use.

How much?

When?

Where?

Other conditions:

❯ Think about your own family and jot down any other techniques for managing these refusals effectively.

▼ 52%

⏱ 10 mins

What to Do When Your Kid Refuses to Eat

❯ What kinds of refusals does your child make when it comes to food?

❯ What food-related rules could you set within your family?

❯ Which of the techniques that you learnt in today's episode could you use?

▼ 56%

🕐 12 mins

How to Handle Separation Anxiety

❯ **Do you feel guilty when you drop off your child at nursery school, at their grandparents' or at a babysitter's?**
Let's take a look at you and at what you're feeling. Write the reasons why you feel this way below.

_____

_____

_____

_____

_____

❯ **What techniques are you going to use to tell your child you'll be leaving them for a while?**

_____

_____

_____

_____

_____

_____

_____

_____

_____

▼ 61%

 11 mins

What to Do If Your Kid Refuses to Do Their Homework

❯ What homework-related rules could you set?

_____

_____

_____

_____

_____

_____

❯ Which of the techniques that you've learnt in this episode will you be able to use to get them to cooperate?

_____

_____

_____

_____

▼ 65%

🕐 5 mins

What to Do If Your Kid Refuses to Pick Up Their Belongings/Tidy Up

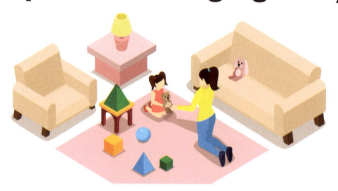

❯ What rules can you set to help your child have less work when things need tidying up?

_____

_____

_____

_____

_____

❯ What other techniques could you personally use to get your child to cooperate in keeping things tidy?

_____

_____

_____

_____

_____

▼ 69%

9 mins

How to Stop Thumb Sucking

❯ **When did your child start sucking their thumb?**

❯ **Write down 5 reasons why it is harmful for your child.** Explain these reasons to them.

_____

_____

_____

_____

_____

❯ **Agree on a code word that you'll use to remind them to take their thumb out of their mouth.**

▼ 74%

🕐 4 mins

When Your Child Refuses to Sleep in Their Own Bed

❯ **When do you plan to start 'training' your child to sleep in their own bed?**
Write the whole plan below, just as you learnt in today's episode.

▼ 78%

4 mins

What to Do When Your Kid Dresses Inappropriately for School

❯ **Set rules or limits concerning your child's clothes.** Write them down here and explain them to your child.

❯ Imagine that your teenager wants to go to school in something you think is too short. What do you say to them?

_____

_____

_____

_____

_____

_____

_____

▼ 82%

Exercise

❯ **Fill in the following table in preparation for Chapter 2.**
Each day, write down some positive and some challenging behaviours and the Need that lies behind each one.

Positive behaviour	Basic Psychological Need

Challenging behaviour	

▼ 87%

Score: /10

What Have You Learnt so Far?

Congratulations! You've completed **Chapter 1.** Take this self-evaluation test to see how well you've taken the information on board. Depending on the result, you'll see whether what you've learnt has sunk in or whether you need to watch some episodes again. Check your answers at the end of the Playbook.

 If you'd like to know your result immediately without having to add up scores, you can take the test **online**. Go to **https://bit.ly/TestChapter1** or scan the QR code.

1. How does a child who has a predominant Need for Relatedness behave?
a. Has frequent tantrums.
b. Is extremely clingy and demands a lot of attention.
c. Refuses to speak to strangers and only wants you.

2. Which Basic Psychological Need isn't being met when a child refuses to try new activities or gives up quickly?
a. The Need for Relatedness — they want you to help them.
b. The Need for Autonomy — they feel like they're losing control and can't cope.
c. The Need for Competence — they feel they can't learn, so they don't even try.

3. What is the parenting style of a parent who always puts their child first, solves all of their issues and never lets them suffer in any way?
a. Balanced — that's how all parents should act.
b. Permissive — the child is not given any responsibility.
c. Authoritarian — the parent knows what is best for their child.

▼ 91%

4. What role do rules play in raising children?

a. They are techniques of authoritarian parents and should be avoided.

b. A balanced upbringing relies on pre-established rules and boundaries.

c. Rules should be as strict as possible.

5. You're going to take your child to the doctor's for an injection. What do you tell them?

a. You prepare them for what is going to happen. You tell them that it will hurt a bit but you don't lie about what will take place.

b. You don't tell them anything and try to distract them when the doctor gives them the injection.

c. You tell them they are a big boy now and only little girls cry. You're making them man up. You won't let them whine. They have to be tough.

6. You're at the table and your child is pestering you for dessert. What do you tell them?

a. You can have some, if you eat up.

b. Yes, after you've finished what's on your plate.

c. You can't have dessert until you've finished eating your dinner.

7. Your teenager wants to go into town on a Tuesday. How do you react?

a. You don't let them go anywhere. They are strictly forbidden from going out on weekdays.

b. They can go out. This is how they practice having responsibility, and they will bear the consequences of their own actions if they're not ready for school tomorrow.

c. 'Yes, you can go out after you've done your homework and if you come home no later than 9 pm.'

▼ 96%

8. Your young child wants to go on the slide by themselves and you don't think it's safe yet. How do you react?

a. You explain that they're still too small to climb the ladder by themselves and then give them a choice: 'Hold my hand while you climb, or shall we go on the swings? You choose.'

b. You take them off the ladder and smack their bottom. They have to learn that they are not allowed to do it.

c. You pick them up and promise to buy them a toy to make them forget about the slide.

9. Which of the consequences below has been applied correctly?

a. 'You've got ice cream on yourself and made a huge mess! Right, no more ice cream this summer!' — Then you take the ice cream out of their hand and throw it in the bin.

b. 'If you choose not to do your homework, you're choosing the possibility of getting a low grade for that class. Is that what you want?'.

c. You let them climb on the furniture. Sure, they run the risk of breaking a limb if they fall, but how else will they learn that they shouldn't do it?

10. Your child has already been watching TV for a while and you think they've had enough for today. What do you do?

a. Grab the remote and switch off the TV. At the end of the day, the remote control is for parents, not kids.

b. Tell them several times, then begin slowly and deliberately counting to 10.

c. Tell them the TV is going off in 10 minutes. When the time is up, tell them that the TV has to to be switched off now. 'I'll let you choose. Either you switch it off, or I do.'

▼ 100%

Notes

" Jot down any other ideas or notes you want to remember
from this chapter.

Chapter 1: The Essentials of Parent-Child Cooperation

2

THE FUNDAMENTALS OF A BALANCED PARENT

Chapter 2 Contents

The Fundamentals of a Balanced Parent

1 min.

Chapter 2 Introduction

01 In this chapter, you'll learn what the **3 Basic Psychological Needs** are and why they are the source of your child's behaviour.

02 We're then going to discuss **parenting styles**, i.e. the reason why what you think and do doesn't exactly match up with what your partner thinks and does. Or your mother-in-law. Or your mum. Or the childminder.

03 Lastly, you'll see how **your child's brain** develops as they grow and what you should be doing at each stage.

 3%

3 mins

Your Responsibility

Realistically speaking, there are only 3 areas in which you really have control.

ACTIONS AND REACTIONS

DECISIONS AND CHOICES

PERCEPTIONS

To increase your spheres of influence, you first need to know how far that influence extends. Focus on what you can actually do.

▶ **Below, make a list of all the things you personally have control over. Where do you have input? In what situations do you make the decisions?**

 6%

🕐 6 mins

Parenting Styles — Introduction

❯ **What were your parents like?**

❯ **Were they more authoritarian or permissive?**

❯ **What was each one's style?**

❯ **Who defended you when you messed up?**

❯ **How did they view mistakes?**

❯ **Who punished you?**

▼ 9%

❯ What impact have the things they did had on you?

❯ How many of these things did you assume were good for you and your child?

❯ Which of these behaviours have you picked up and now use yourself, as a parent?

❯ Which of them would you like to change?

▼ 12%

🕐 9 mins

The Authoritarian Parent

> Authoritarian parents often use 'have to' because, with them, it's my way or the highway. They are too strict and very rarely gentle. They set clear, inflexible limits that must not be broken.

❯ Who in your family is an authoritarian parent? Maybe it's you?
❯ Now that you know the long-term effects of this style of parenting, which typically authoritarian traits will you keep and which ones will you change?
Write them below.

_____

_____

_____

_____

_____

▼ 15%

The Permissive Parent

> 'I'll give my kids what I didn't have'.
> 'I wasn't allowed to do anything, so you can do what you want!'
> There are no consequences for challenging behaviour.
> There are never any limits.
> They are gentle, sometimes firm, but never consistent.

❯ Were your parents permissive? _____

❯ What permissive behaviour do you currently display towards your child? _____

_____

_____

_____

_____

▼ 18%

The Balanced Parent — Part I

> **Below, fill in the convictions of a balanced parent, according to the explanations in the video episode.**

At a certain point, your child will spread their wings. Tread their own path. They will have to solve problems by themselves and make their own rules.

Loving a child means commitment and accepting everything about them, regardless of what they do. Love is not given or taken. Love just is.

The other person has their own decisions and choices to make. You cannot force somebody to make a choice, to be creative or to love.

It is not the parent who is more important, as the authoritarian parent believes, nor the child, as the permissive parent believes. We are simply in the same family and equally important.

Balanced parents understand that their child is in the process of learning, and they use mistakes to enhance this process.

 21%

Parents establish boundaries and values which they convey clearly to their children and to other people around them.

The way in which we act is influenced by what we think. But we can control both these things.

The Balanced Parent makes decisions together with their child and involves the child in activities. The key word is 'together' — learning how to work as a team.

The Balanced Parent works continuously on their own emotions, mental patterns and behaviours.

The Balanced Parent does not compare their child to other children, and they understand that 'success' means being the best version of yourself.

▼ 24%

" Children need boundaries! Be both firm and loving.

❯ **Write down the characteristics of a Balanced Parent.**

_____

_____

_____

❯ **Take a look at your own convictions, actions and perceptions. Which characteristics of the Balanced Parenting Style have you discovered?**

_____

_____

_____

27%

🕐 10 mins

Parenting Styles — Examples and Situations

The Authoritarian Parent
Usually threatens and punishes.
Children listen out of fear.

The Permissive Parent
Does nothing. Wants an easy life.
Children are unruly.

The Balanced Parent
Plans ahead. Empathises with their child, talks to them and gives them
limits and options. Within these limits, a child can make decisions, have
choices and give their point of view.

▼ 29%

🕐 8 mins

Different Parenting Styles

 The responsibility for making changes lies with you. **You cannot force others to change** their behaviour. When your partner has an extreme parenting style, **you need to adopt the middle ground** for there to be balance in the family. **Become a role model**, even if your other half goes from one extreme to the other!

❯ Think about the **differences in parenting styles** between other members of your family. Take a few common situations and fill in the table below. **What would be the middle ground that you could agree on to bring some balance?**

What do you do?	What does your partner do?	What do the grandparents do?	What does _____ do?	The middle ground

▼ 32%

🕐 10 mins

Grandparents, Nannies, Teachers

 Lead by example!
Choose some rules that are important to you. You want the other person to understand and follow them. Give that person the space to make decisions or suggest alternatives that would work for your child.

▶ Write down the rules for your child that are non-negotiable below.

▼ 35%

🕐 5 mins

Your Child as a Grown-Up

❯ You knock on the door and your child answers. They are 30. What do they look like? Visualise a mental picture and describe them here. What qualities does your child have?

❯ What principles have they adopted?

_____

_____

_____

_____

_____

❯ Describe their characteristics. What's their life like overall?

_____

_____

_____

_____

_____

_____

_____

❯ Which of these characteristics do you both share? ❯ Which don't you have but would like to acquire?

▼ 41%

🕐 4 mins

The Challenges You Face Today

> Which behaviours from the list you made at the start are a priority for you to fix?

_____

_____

_____

_____

> Use the space below to write down the problems that will arise as your child grows up.

_____

_____

_____

_____

_____

_____

_____

_____

_____

▼ 44%

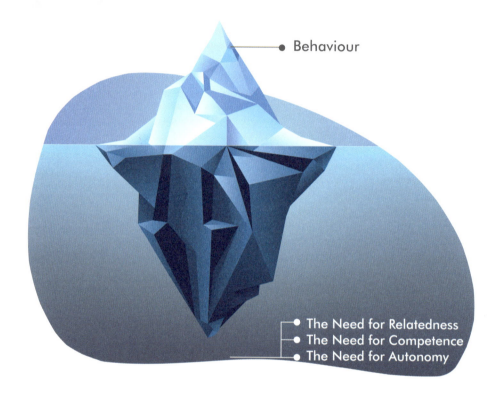

Behaviour

The Need for Relatedness
The Need for Competence
The Need for Autonomy

Needs generate thoughts, thoughts generate emotions and sentiments, and these then materialise as behaviour.

From today, rather than reacting to your child's behaviour, I encourage you to think about the Need that lies behind it.

To correct your child's challenging behaviour, give them what they need as much as possible.
You'll find out how to do so in the next chapters.

▼ 47%

Episode 15

10 mins

B.F. Skinner's Theory

> B.F. Skinner was a behavioural psychologist who developed the reinforcement theory in the '60s. The theory states that the only 2 mechanisms that motivate humans to demonstrate or refrain from a behaviour are punishment and reward.

▶ What happens in the long run if we get the child to 'cooperate' based on punishment and reward?

_____

_____

_____

_____

_____

▶ What will the adult who has been educated mainly on the basis of punishment and reward be like?

_____

_____

_____

_____

_____

▼ 50%

🕐 7 mins

The 3 Basic Psychological Needs — Introduction

As we go through life, we all try to fulfil the 3 Basic Psychological Needs in everything we do.

Need for _____

The need to give just as much as you receive. The need to feel that you are heard, respected and valued. The need to love and be loved unconditionally.

Need for _____

The need to learn, develop and be capable. I need to feel that I can.

Need for _____

The need to make decisions and have choices. I need to be the source of my actions.

▼ 53%

5 mins

The Need for Relatedness

Behaviours through which a child tries to fulfil the Need for Relatedness	
Positive	Challenging

The Need for Competence

Behaviours through which a child tries to fulfil the Need for Competence	
Positive	Challenging

5 mins

The Need for Autonomy

Behaviours through which a child tries to fulfil the Need for Autonomy	
Positive	Challenging

A State of Balance

❯ **In order to experience balance, these 3 Needs must all be fulfilled. However, each person's dominant need will vary.**
Write the name of your child under the picture that represents what you believe is their predominant need at the moment.

| THE NEED FOR RELATEDNESS | THE NEED FOR COMPETENCE | THE NEED FOR AUTONOMY |

Because the Basic Psychological Needs are like a hunger, they need daily, consistent and continuous effort to remain balanced.

In the following episodes, you will see what you can do to fulfil each of these 3 Needs in your child.

▼ 66%

9 mins

The Domino Effect

" If just one of the 3 Needs is not met, it will have a knock-on effect on the others.

❯ Think about the challenging behaviours your child has displayed in the past week. Sort these behaviours according to the Need that they're trying to fulfil with each behaviour.

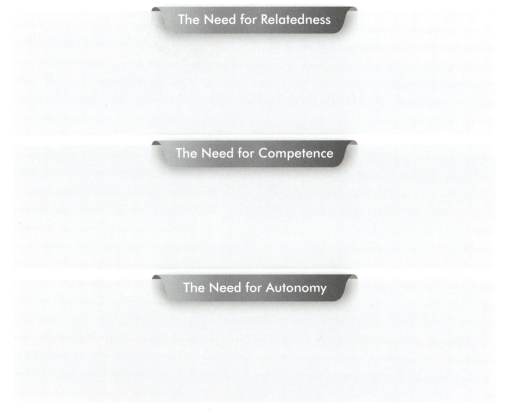

The Need for Relatedness

The Need for Competence

The Need for Autonomy

▼ 69%

🕐 7 mins

How Your Child's Brain Develops

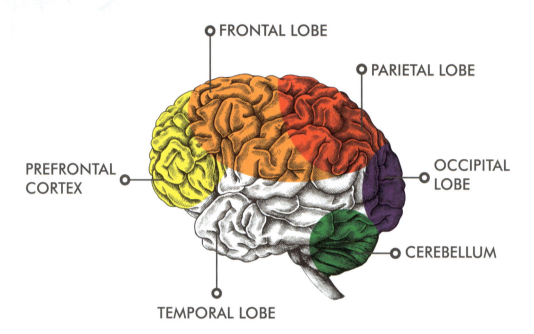

FRONTAL LOBE

PARIETAL LOBE

PREFRONTAL CORTEX

OCCIPITAL LOBE

CEREBELLUM

TEMPORAL LOBE

❯ Which information in this episode sparked an 'aha!' moment about your child's development?

▼ 71%

🕐 8 mins

How to Manage Screen Time

 For a child to be attentive and able to concentrate, they need to do as many cognitive activities **as possible**. Access to screens and gadgets should be kept to a minimum, with none at all for **0- to 3-year-olds**. Try to really limit the use of televisions and screens of any kind.

Does your child watch too much television? Are they always asking for the tablet or phone? Before giving in, ask yourself the following questions:

❯ How often is my child using the tablet, TV or other device at the moment?

❯ What will happen to my child's brain and development in the long term?

❯ Should I be saying 'no'?

❯ Do they really need another app or game?

❯ What's my limit going to be?

Don't forget, you're the one holding the remote!

▼ 74%

How Children Think

Children live in the present.

Children look for the fun in everything.

Until the age of 7, they learn in terms of cause and effect. They don't have a sense of awareness.

Children think in 'black and white'. They cannot understand abstract concepts.

▼ 77%

🕐 7 mins

How Your Child Develops from 0-3

 A child's wants are, in fact, their needs.
When they express something they want, it is actually an expression of need. This is why babies cannot be spoiled.
Children have a great Need for physical Relatedness!

❯ **Write down how a baby's Need for Relatedness manifests itself.**

❯ In the period from 12 months to 3 years old, what are the most common Needs?

_____

_____

_____

❯ Write down how these Needs manifest themselves, using your own experience with your child or the explanations in this episode.

_____

_____

_____

_____

_____

_____

_____

_____

_____

_____

_____

▼ 83%

5 mins

How Your Child Develops from 3-18

❯ Which Need comes up the most between the ages of 3 and 6? What can you do to make sure you don't stifle this Need?

_____

_____

_____

_____

_____

_____

_____

_____

_____

❯ Which measures should you take for this age group (3-6) in relation to the Need for Autonomy?

_____

_____

_____

_____

_____

_____

_____

_____

▼ 87%

> For each age group, write down the challenges that are likely to arise around each of the 3 Basic Psychological Needs.

As well as the information from the episode, add your own observations if you've already been through this stage with your child.

	The Need for Relatedness	The Need for Competence	The Need for Autonomy
6-8 years			
9-11 years			
12-14 years			
15-18 years			

▼ 90%

Score: /10

What Have You Learnt so Far?

Congratulations!
You've completed **Chapter 2**.
Take this self-evaluation test to see how well you've taken on board the information we've shared with you. Depending on the result, you'll see whether what you've learnt has sunk in or whether you need to watch some episodes again. Check your answers at the end of the Playbook.

 If you'd like to know your result immediately without having to add up scores, you can take the test **online**. Go to **https://bit.ly/TestChapter2** or scan the QR code.

1. **How can you get the most out of the All About Parenting programme?**
a. Schedule a time and place for watching the episodes.
b. Do the exercises and homework.
c. Work through all the episodes to get all the information.

2. **The problems you currently have with your child...**
a. Can be resolved with a few magic words.
b. Are actually just a symptom.
c. Show how stubborn they are. They take after their other parent.

3. **Which of the opinions below are the convictions of an Authoritarian Parent?**
a. Any decision regarding their child is up to them.
b. Children must listen to their parents. No exceptions.
c. Breaking the rules shows a lack of respect.
d. 'Spare the rod and spoil the child.'
e. Children can have opinions about decisions taken as a household.
f. Children need to be supervised and controlled.

▼ 93%

4. Which of the opinions below are the convictions of a Permissive Parent?

a. The most important person in the family is the parent themselves.
b. They instantly comply with their child's wants.
c. There are no consequences for challenging behaviour.
d. Outside factors cause challenging behaviour in children.
e. Children make choices in all areas of their lives.
f. They would leave a child crying because they want an easy life.

5. Which of the opinions below are the convictions of a Balanced Parent?

a. Children need boundaries.
b. Parents need to be both firm and loving.
c. It's okay for parents to break the rules as long as the child follows them.
d. All members of the family are equally important and should be treated with the same respect.
e. A balanced parent is a role model for their child.
f. A balanced parent believes that rights come with responsibilities.

6. How do Balanced Parents handle mistakes?

a. Punish the child.
b. Let nature take its course, whatever the situation.
c. They believe a child shouldn't suffer.
d. Treat mistakes as a learning opportunity.

7. What do you do if the other parent's parenting style differs from yours?

a. Do all that you can to impose your point of view on them.
b. Go to the other extreme to balance out the situation.
c. Make yourself an example of balanced behaviour.

▼ 97%

8. Which Basic Psychological Need is manifested when a child cries at nursery school?

a. Autonomy — they need to calm down by themselves.

b. Competence — give them the space to do activities and learn.

c. Relatedness — hug them and empathise with them.

9. Which Basic Psychological Need is usually manifested in a child who refuses everything?

a. Relatedness — they need to receive what they want and feel loved.

b. Autonomy — the only way to feel they have control is to refuse to cooperate.

c. Competence — they want to see how loud they can shout.

10. Which Basic Psychological Need is a child displaying when they are constantly 'acting up' and always looking for something new to try?

a. Relatedness — they want to get your attention with all their shenanigans.

b. Autonomy — they want to demonstrate that they have control.

c. Competence — they want to learn new things and see how much they can do.

▼ 100%

Notes

Jot down any other ideas or notes
you want to remember from this chapter here.

Chapter 2: The Fundamentals of a Balanced Parent

Chapter 2: The Fundamentals of a Balanced Parent

3

SELF-ESTEEM AND OPTIMAL MOTIVATION

Chapter 3 Contents

Self-Esteem and Optimal Motivation

🕐 1 min.

Chapter 3 Introduction

 01 What does success mean?

 03 Why kids say 'I don't want to'.

 02 What is optimal and suboptimal motivation?

 04 How to encourage your child to achieve.

 2%

🕐 5 mins

What is Self-Esteem?

❯ Try this exercise for yourself.
Stand in front of the mirror and see how you feel about yourself.
Answer the following questions on a scale of 1-10.

1. Do I like myself as I am?

2. How do I rate myself?

3. How worthy of respect do I consider myself?

4. How worthy of love do I consider myself?

5. How much value do I think I have?

6. How much do I value myself as an individual?

Work out the average. What is my overall Self-Esteem like?

SCORE:

▼ 5%

Image-Esteem

 Self-Esteem is the link between your feelings and your own persona. Image-Esteem refers to the way in which other **people's perceptions** of you influence the image you have of yourself.

> Repeat the exercise from the previous episode.
> Stand in front of the mirror and answer the following questions:

1. What opinion do others have of me?

1 2 3 4 5 6 7 8 9 10

2. How do others rate me?

1 2 3 4 5 6 7 8 9 10

3. How worthy of respect am I in the eyes of those around me?

1 2 3 4 5 6 7 8 9 10

4. How worthy of love do others consider me?

1 2 3 4 5 6 7 8 9 10

5. How much value do others think I have?

1 2 3 4 5 6 7 8 9 10

▼ 7%

6. How much do others value me as an individual?

Work out the average. What is my overall Image-Esteem like?

SCORE:

❯ Does the way others perceive you have any bearing on the way in which you perceive yourself?

_____

_____

❯ Do you feel like your real value comes from the perceptions of those around you?

_____

_____

❯ What happens to your self-perception when it is not validated by those outside?

_____

_____

_____

▼ 10%

7 mins

Ego-Esteem / Egocentrism

 When a child receives too much praise, they start to believe that they are the bee's knees. These children will always feel **the need to show others** that they are the best. They'll always want to be the first, at the front, and have all eyes on them.

1. Which one of the statements below is false?

a. Someone who is constantly seeking validation has high Image-Esteem.
T / F

b. The higher your Self-Esteem, the higher your need for validation.
T / F

c. Egocentric behaviour stems from fragile Self-Esteem.
T / F

2. A child who is always in your face and competitive always has overinflated:

a. Self-Esteem
b. Image-Esteem

3. How does someone become egocentric?

a. Their Self-Esteem gets too high.
b. From being excessively praised.
c. It's just only children who can be egocentric.

 ▼ 12%

🕐 7 mins

Traits of Someone With Low Self-Esteem

❯ Circle the statements that apply to somebody with low Self-Esteem.

a. Greets new challenges with fear/enthusiasm.
b. 'It's not my fault I didn't succeed. Things were against me.'/'It's my fault when things don't turn out well. I just need to try harder.'
c. They fight for their rights/won't ask for what's rightfully theirs.
d. Settles for 'good enough'/is conscientious and pro-active.

❯ Take a look at the image below. What areas would a person with low Self-Esteem focus on most?

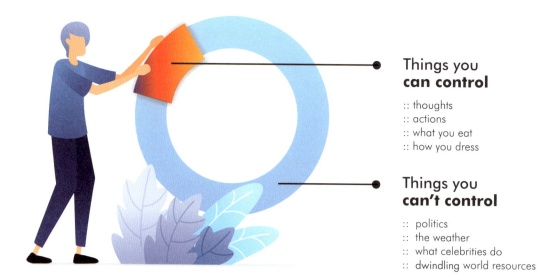

Things you can control

:: thoughts
:: actions
:: what you eat
:: how you dress

Things you can't control

:: politics
:: the weather
:: what celebrities do
:: dwindling world resources

▼ 15%

🕐 11 mins

Traits of Someone With High Self-Esteem

❯ How do the 3 Basic Psychological Needs manifest themselves in relation to Self-Esteem? Fill out the table below using what you learnt today.

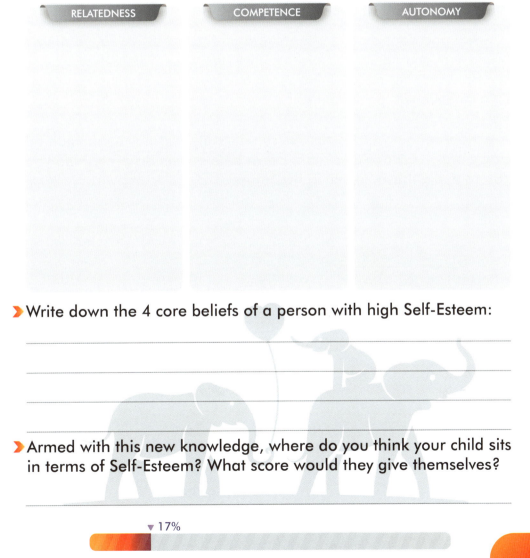

RELATEDNESS	COMPETENCE	AUTONOMY

❯ Write down the 4 core beliefs of a person with high Self-Esteem:

❯ Armed with this new knowledge, where do you think your child sits in terms of Self-Esteem? What score would they give themselves?

▼ 17%

🕐 5 mins

Irony and Self-Esteem

❯ **What does a child hear when their parents make fun of them?**
  a. They laugh; it's only a joke.
  b. They get angry. They understand the irony and they don't like it.
  c. They feel inadequate, unloved and like they're in the way.

❯ **At what age does a child understand all the words we say to them?**
  a. From around 12 months (or when they start talking themselves).
  b. From birth (they are assimilating words even from within the womb).
  c. From 8 months.

❯ **Are there certain words you use in your family that may be considered ironic or sarcastic? Write them down below, then do everything you can to avoid these 'jokes' in the future.**

HA
HA

▼ 19%

🕐 9 mins

Labels

 If I tell a child 'You're naughty', they'll be naughty, because they act up according to the label that's been put on them.

❯ **Think of all of the behaviours that you would like your child to demonstrate. Do you want them to be generous? Hard-working? A good team player? Write them below.**

_____

_____

_____

Find solutions for the following scenarios:
Remember: In order to discourage Image-Esteem, avoid superlatives such as 'You are the best at sharing'.

❯ **Replace the negative labels below with positives:**

'Don't be spoilt!'

'You're being such a naughty boy, stop hitting!'

❯ **How do you discourage labels that other people might try to use?**

'I didn't know you were so shy, Seth!'

'You must be so proud of her. She's so beautiful, isn't she?'

'Matthew, you're a very cheeky young man!'

▼ 22%

🕐 6 mins

Comparisons

❝ Comparisons feed children's Image-Esteem.

❯ **What are the long-term consequences of using comparisons?**

_____   _____

_____   _____

_____   _____

❯ **Rephrase the following statements to remove the comparisons**
'Put your jacket back on. Do you see any other children here in just a T-shirt?'

_____

'Sit still. Do you see anyone else running around the restaurant?'

_____

❯ **Have you ever used comparisons to encourage your child to behave in a certain way?**
Write down those situations. Now you'll remember them next time they come up and will be able to phrase your request differently.

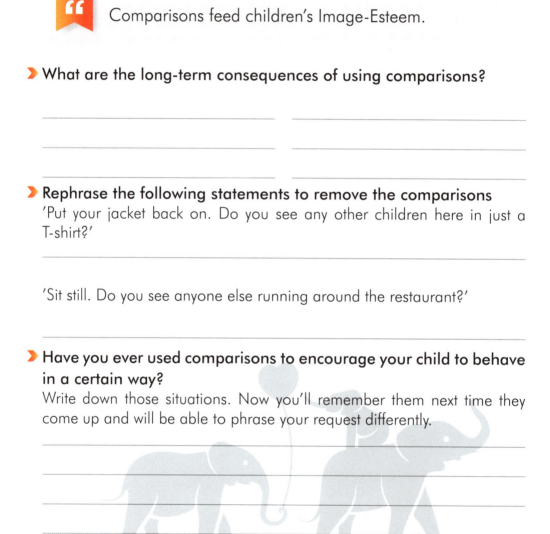

▼ 24%

Chapter 3: Self-Esteem and Optimal Motivation

Expressions and Feelings to Avoid

Humiliation • Guilt • Shame • Fear

 Humiliation is one of the most hurtful ways of destroying Self-Esteem.

▶ **What are the most common forms of humiliation?**
Write them below.

_____

_____

▶ **What do children understand when they hear their parents saying, 'If you don't come with me now, I'm going to leave you here!'**
a. Oh, mum is tired. I should hurry up.
b. If I don't do what mum says, I could be abandoned at any time.

▶ **What are the consequences of this phrase in the long run?**
a. On a future romantic relationship.

_____

b. On the relationship with their parents.

_____

▶ **Which of the Basic Psychological Needs are affected when we use phrases like:**
'You disappoint me!' 'You're embarrassing me.' 'You're good for nothing!'

a. The Need for Relatedness.
b. The Need for Competence.
c. The Need for Autonomy.

▼ 27%

⏱ 7 mins

Unconditional Love

❝ 'No matter how you behave, the path you follow in life or the choices you make, **I love you just as you are**.'

❯ **Choose the true statements of unconditional love from the options below.**

a. 'I'm not talking to you because you're not doing things the way I tell you'.

b. 'I'm writing you out of my will'/'You're no longer my child.'

c. 'I love you, whatever you decide.'

d. 'The most important thing for me is that you are happy with your own choices.'

e. Too much love goes to your head and you become spoilt.

f. Showing love is healthy.

g. 'I'm holding back displays of affection to punish you for what you did wrong.'

h. I say 'I love you' as a reward.

i. Unconditional love is when you feel loved in all circumstances, not just when you're the best version of yourself.

▼ 29%

 11 mins

Sharing Parents' Love

 Children measure love by the time that you spend with them.

▶ **Do the following activity with your children.**
Let them do the colouring in.
Draw the flower and talk about the love you share between your children, just as you learnt in the episode.

Use the following words:
'Each of you was born with love inside you. I love you both/all equally, but in different ways, because you are different.'

Show your children you love them by spending time separately with each of them.

▶ **Schedule some special time to spend with each of your children and write it down below.**

Special time with _____ **Special time with** _____
When?   When?

🕐 11 mins

Avoid Punishment

❯ **What do children think when you put them on the 'naughty step', or in 'time out'?**

    a. I've been naughty/I've made a mistake. Next time, I'll do better.
    b. It's not right that I'm sitting here.
    c. I have to calm down. I will use this time to breathe deeply and
       have a think.

❯ **What kind of activities can we use to really calm children down?**
Write down some activities they like that might calm them down.

_____

_____

_____

_____

❯ **Imagine the following situation. Your child gets angry and you don't like the way they are behaving.**
Write down what you could say rather than punishing them, using what you learnt in today's episode.

_____

_____

_____

_____

_____

▼ 34%

8 mins

Perfectionism

❯ Your child was supposed to have tidied their room but there are still clothes all over the floor. On the next page, fill in the replies you could give, using the example below:

'Wow, you've dressed yourself! I think it's great that you can dress yourself, don't you? Does it feel good to be able to dress yourself? Look! You put your trousers on properly. They're the right way round. Your socks match. That's so great! Well 90% is really well done, isn't it? Let's see what we can do about this jumper. Does anything seem wrong with this jumper to you?'

Look for positives

01

02

03

04

Address problems tactfully and focus on learning, not the mistake

Ask them how they feel while doing it

Describe what's been done well

▼ 36%

_____
_____
_____
_____
_____
_____
_____
_____
_____
_____
_____
_____
_____
_____

❯ Think of other similar situations that you have faced. Describe how you might react next time in a way that keeps your child's Self-Esteem intact.

_____
_____
_____
_____
_____
_____
_____
_____

▼ 39%

🕐 4 mins

Notice Them Doing Good

❯ **Write down the behaviours that you would like to see more often from your child.**

Every time you see them doing one of these things, be sure to say something about it. Praise them. Thank them. **e.g.** They put a plate in the sink, take something to the bin, etc.

_____

_____

_____

_____

_____

_____

_____

_____

_____

_____

_____

To improve your relationship, every day, tell yourself that you will say 'thank you', 'I like that' and 'I'm thankful for' to the people in your life at least 3 times.

▼ 41%

🕐 6 mins

Let Them Dream

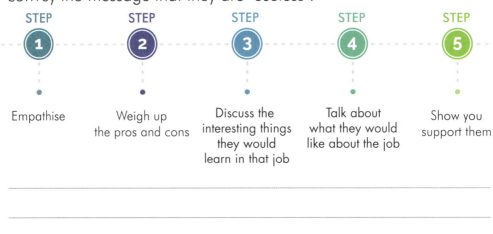

> **What 'impossible' or 'absurd' job does your child want to do when they're older?** Using what you learnt in today's episode, write down the conversation you might have with them in a way that doesn't convey the message that they are 'useless'.

STEP **1**	STEP **2**	STEP **3**	STEP **4**	STEP **5**
Empathise	Weigh up the pros and cons	Discuss the interesting things they would learn in that job	Talk about what they would like about the job	Show you support them

_____

_____

_____

_____

▼ 44%

> What did you want to be when you were a child?

> How did the people around you react when you told them?

> How did you feel?

> How close is your actual career to what you wanted to do when you were a child?

▼ 46%

🕐 9 mins

Mistakes Are Learning Opportunities

❯ Imagine a situation in which your child has made a big mistake. Follow the steps below and have a conversation with them so as to shorten the learning process and make sure that next time, they'll know to do things differently.

1. Empathise

2. Ask questions about what happened

3. Teach them how to do things correctly. Show them the process!

4. Find opportunities to put this into practice

5. Make sure they CAN do it

6. Make sure they KNOW HOW to do it

▼ 49%

🕐 3 mins

Discover Their Opinion

❯ Why is it important to ask your child's opinion?

_____

_____

❯ How does a child feel when they're asked for their opinion about a situation?

_____

_____

❯ Think of a few scenarios in which you could ask for your child's opinion. Take into account some of the upcoming events in your life.

_____

_____

_____

_____

_____

_____

_____

_____

_____

▼ 51%

🕐 4 mins

It's Their Room and Their Clothes

❯ In this episode, you saw how important it is to let your child dress the way they want to. Write a few of the reasons why below.

_____

_____

❯ What limits can you set on cost or decency for both your child's room and their clothes?

_____

_____

_____

_____

_____

▼ 53%

🕐 10 mins

Stop Praising.
Ask Questions and Describe

❯ Why is it unhelpful to just say to a child 'Well done', 'Wow', 'That was incredible', etc.? What are the consequences?

1. You increase _____ Esteem but not _____ Esteem

2. Praise generates optimal/suboptimal motivation.

3. Praise generates an excessive desire for _____ from outside.

❯ Imagine that your child comes to show you something they've done, e.g. a puzzle they've just finished.
Ask them questions based on the examples you learnt today.

❝ **Ask them about:**
    1. How they felt while doing the activity.
    2. How they did it.
    3. How they feel about the result.

1. _____

2. _____

3. _____

   _____

▼ 56%

🕐 9 mins

Healthy vs Unhealthy Competition

❯ **Link the statement on the right with the type of competition.**

UNHEALTHY COMPETITION

a. praise success at the end

b. break down objectives into small steps

c. you have to be better than the others

d. sometimes, you can only go so far

e. focus on what they've already learnt

f. be better than you were the day before

HEALTHY COMPETITION

g. praise successes at every stage

h. there's no such thing as 'I can't'

i. focus on what's left to do

j. look at the objective as a whole

▼ 58%

8 mins

Competition vs Cooperation

> **In what context is competition healthy?**

The players are:

The rules are:

The results are:

> **What would you say to a child who is entering a competition?**
Choose the right option

a. 'If you choose to play, it means that you're choosing the possibility that you might lose. If you're prepared to play, you're prepared to lose. And I might lose this game, just like you might lose.'
b. 'Give everything you have and you'll succeed. If you work hard, you'll win! There's no way you can lose now. That's not a possibility.'

> **What does a child need to know about cooperation?**
What questions are you going to ask them to help them understand whether the process they've started is a competition or not and how to take the most from it?

▼ 61%

The Dolphin Training Technique

❯ **Fill in the table below.**

Then use one colour to highlight the expressions that you use yourself. Use another colour for the ones you want to give up, based on what you've learnt so far.

Advice	How it's helped you

What Performance Really Means

▶ **Sketch out your child's achievement.**

What things do they do in line with what you'd expect? Where are they exceeding expectations or are better than others? What are the problem areas?

Encourage them in the areas where they have more difficulties. Don't compare their achievements to those of others.

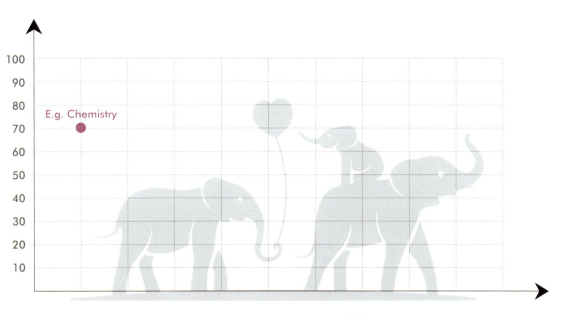

E.g. Chemistry

▼ 66%

Chapter 3: Self-Esteem and Optimal Motivation

❯ You can repeat this graph for each of your children. You can also repeat the exercise once you've put the methods for achievement in place, to see how you've progressed since today.

There are 3 conditions for any activity to be fulfilled:

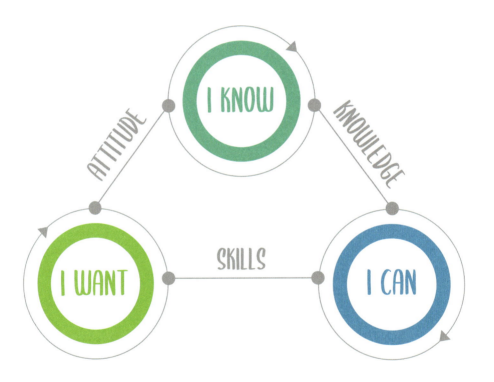

If achievement is substandard, then the child either doesn't know, can't or doesn't want to. Find the causes behind your child's lack of achievement.

▼ 68%

A New Perspective on Motivation

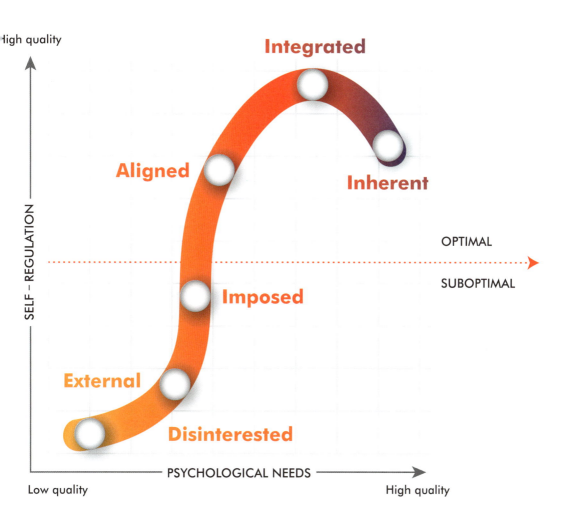

Motivation chart — Susan Fowler

Keep this chart at hand. It will be useful in the coming episodes.

▼ 70%

🕐 4 mins

Disinterested Motivation

 Disinterested Motivation manifests when you feel that something you have to do doesn't fulfil any of **the 3 Basic Psychological Needs:** the Need for Competence, the Need for Relatedness and the Need for Autonomy.

❯ **Fill in the table below with some of the activities where you and your child display this type of motivation.**

e.g. Writing a report that you know nobody will read

e.g. Cleaning out the wardrobe

▼ 73%

5 mins

External Motivation

 External Motivation is when you feel you need something or someone from outside to motivate you to do a certain task or activity. You receive either a bribe or praise.

❯ Fill in the table below with some of the activities where you and your child display this type of motivation.

e.g. I'll get a bonus if I finish the project on time.

e.g. They'll get a new bike if they get all A's.

▼ 75%

🕐 5 mins

Imposed Motivation

> This motivation stems from fear. In other words, you're doing what you're doing because you fear punishment or other negative consequences.

▶ **Fill in the table below with some of the activities where you and your child display this type of motivation.**

e.g. I'll get a fine if I break the speed limit.

e.g. If they don't eat all their dinner up, they can't watch cartoons.

▼ 78%

7 mins

Aligned Motivation

 Aligned Motivation is when you feel that what you are doing is related to an objective, conviction or principle that you believe in and that is important for you.

❯ **Fill in the table below with some of the activities where you display this type of motivation. What are the principles related to these behaviours?** e.g. I always arrive on time — punctuality

_____

_____

_____

❯ **Write activities that your child doesn't enjoy doing in the column on the left. Then link them to the principle that you'd like your child to have. Over the course of this programme, you will discover a routine for this and how to implement it.**

Activities they don't like doing	Belief / Principle

▼ 80%

🕐 5 mins

Integrated Motivation

" Integrated Motivation leads to performance. It is linked with activities that you do gladly and enthusiastically. If you could do only that, you would do it all day long.

❯ **Fill in the table below with some of the activities where you and your child display this type of motivation.**

e.g. I organise all the drawers at home really well.

e.g. They really enjoy drawing.

▼ 83%

4 mins

Inherent Motivation

 When we speak about Inherent Motivation, we're referring to things you can't stop yourself from doing. There is a fine line between enthusiasm and addiction.

❯ **Fill in the table below with some of the activities where you display this type of motivation. e.g.** I can read for hours on end.

_____

_____

_____

❯ Naturally, your child displays inherent motivation in certain activities. Write them in the left-hand column.
Next to them, write the activities they like least and which could be combined with the enjoyable ones to make them easier to do.

Activity done through inherent motivation	Tasks they don't like doing

▼ 85%

Score: /10

What Have You Learnt so Far?

Congratulations!
You've completed **Chapter 3**.
Take this self-evaluation test to see how well you've taken on board the information we've shared with you. Depending on the result, you'll see whether what you've learnt has sunk in or whether you need to watch some episodes again. Check your answers at the end of the Playbook.

 If you'd like to know your result immediately without having to add up scores, you can take the test **online**. Go to **https://bit.ly/Testchapter3** or scan the QR code.

1. Link the concepts on the left to the right statements in the box.

SELF-ESTEEM

IMAGE-ESTEEM

a. A combination of self-belief and respect for oneself

b. Overly concerned with what others think

c. We are born with Optimal _____

d. Considers every action through their own eyes

e. Considers every action through the eyes of others

f. When I look at myself and like myself as I am

g. Validation comes from outside

h. Overinflated _____ leads to egocentrism

▼ 87%

2. Pick the statements that apply to somebody with low Self-Esteem.
a. The lower your Self-Esteem, the higher your need for validation.
b. This kind of person knows their limits.
c. They get no satisfaction from a job well done.
d. They absolutely love compliments.
e. They find excuses for their failures.
f. They think they are not capable.
g. They only accept positive results and reject negative ones.
h. People with low Self-Esteem are introverted.

3. Pick the statements that apply to somebody with high Self-Esteem.
a. They focus more on things within their control.
b. They want to change the world and talk about politics and global warming.
c. They take the minimum amount of risk to be sure that everything works out fine.
d. They find excuses for their failures.
e. They think they are not capable.
f. They only accept positive results and reject negative ones.
g. Their 3 Basic Psychological Needs are met.
h. They feel competent and comfortable in what they're doing.

▼ 90%

4. Read the expressions below carefully, then write them in the correct column.

Why can't you just be a good student, like your sister? • I love you just the way you are. • Wow, so clever — in a sarcastic way. • I know you're a good boy. • Naughty child! • That's how he is, he's shy. • I believe in you. You can sort this argument out with your words. • Can you see any other children running around the restaurant? • You didn't behave very well just then. • What grades did everyone else get? • I love you no matter what you do. • I'm ashamed of you! • I like being with you. • If you don't come with me now, I'm going to leave you here! • I love you equally, but in different ways, because you're different. • Every person is unique.

EXPRESSIONS TO AVOID	EXPRESSIONS TO KEEP

▼ 92%

5. What is the truth about the 'naughty step' at nursery school?

a. Children need to sit still for a while to calm down.

b. It only increases frustration in an already negative situation.

c. If a child feels humiliated, they won't make the same mistake again.

6. How do you calm down an agitated child who is refusing to cooperate?

a. They need space. Send them to their room to calm down by themselves.

b. Use empathy. Nourish their Basic Psychological Needs. Give them options: 'I can see you're angry right now. I care about you and I want you to calm down in a way that makes you feel better. Do you want to draw or come and have a cuddle?'

c. Children can't calm down on command. Leave them in peace until they're back to normal.

7. How can you encourage a child to practice a sport, learn to play an instrument, tidy their room or do their homework?

a. Offer rewards as long as they make an effort and try their best.

b. Limit their access to screens if they affect their concentration.

c. Combine these activities with the ones they enjoy.

d. Speak to their teacher and ask them to spend more time with your child.

8. What are labels and what impact do they have on children (you're lazy/hard-working, you're sensible/naughty, etc.)?

a. Describing a quality or a fault that we see in our children and that becomes a label for those around them.

b. Negative behaviour that we want to correct. Saying it out loud helps with awareness of the problem.

c. A succinct description of the child's personality. Once you've made it clear, no one will be surprised.

▼ 95%

9. Your child is quiet and avoids talking to new people, but they're lively and communicative with people they already know. What is the cause and what could you do?

a. They're shy. Take them out of their comfort zone and force them to do new things.

b. They're probably introverted. They need to be around extroverted friends who'll encourage them to be more talkative.

c. They're probably introverted. If their Self-Esteem is at an optimal level, there is no need to do anything except love them as they are.

10. What do you need to do if you want to increase your child's achievements?

a. Push them to study all subjects, especially where they are weakest. If they can't put in the extra work, they're not going to excel.

b. There's no such thing as 'can't'. They don't have good enough grades to deserve TV or other pointless activities. Ban them from everything until they show they're applying themselves enough at school.

c. Set some limits based on their achievements; organise extra tutoring in the areas where they excel.

▼ 100%

Notes

> Jot down any other ideas or notes you want to remember from this chapter here.

Chapter 3: Self-Esteem and Optimal Motivation

Notes

Notes

Chapter 3: Self-Esteem and Optimal Motivation

4

A COMPETENT CHILD
IS A RESPONSIBLE CHILD

Chapter 4 Contents

A Competent Child Is a Responsible Child

Chapter 4 Description

 01 You're going to learn what competence is.

 02 How you can be a role model for your child so that they know, can and want to.

 03 We'll talk about the Need for Autonomy in the context of responsibility.

 04 What is responsibility and how many types are there?

▼ 3%

🕐 7 mins

The Need for Autonomy and the Definition of Responsibility

 A child develops a sense of responsibility when they are allowed to experiment and do certain things by themselves. This is very closely linked to their Need for Autonomy. It is important to give them freedom within a controlled setting.

▶ **Write down the things you do for your child even though they could do them by themselves.**
If you have more than one child, write what you do for each one.
e.g. I wash the dishes, but he could do that. I tie her laces, even though at her age she could learn to do that on her own.

Make the decision that things will change. You're going to learn clear techniques for making that change in this chapter.

▼ 6%

 11 mins

Balance, Autonomy and Parenting Styles

❯ Put the statements below in the correct category.

A. Offers total freedom, boundaries are very broad.

B. Knows that they have to teach aptitude.

C. Believes that children are not old enough to be offered freedom.

D. Is continually re-calibrating the limits and freedoms that they grant their child, according to what the child knows and can do.

E. If you give a child total freedom, they will learn to be self-reliant.

F. Children can do more than they're allowed to do.

G. Each stage comes with certain limits; as the child grows, the limits increase.

H. Doesn't give their child freedom because they haven't demonstrated the necessary aptitude.

AUTHORITARIAN PARENT	BALANCED PARENT	PERMISSIVE PARENT

▼ 10%

▶ **What age-appropriate freedom could you offer your child? Analyse the situation below and fill in the table with the limits and responsibilities that you would grant.**

Scenario	Limits to impose	Responsibilities
• Crossing the street by themselves	• Only the roads in the neighbourhood, not main streets	• Make sure there are no cars coming before crossing
• Wants to go to a summer camp	• I have to know all the rules at this summer camp	• Listen to the adults in charge, know what to do in an emergency, etc.

🕐 4 mins

The Triangle of Competence

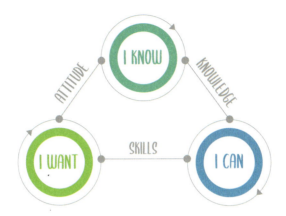

Here is what a child needs in order to carry out an action:

1. Opportunity   2. Knowledge   3. Ability   4. Motivation

❯ **Think of 2 skills you'd like your child to demonstrate.** Fill in as many spaces as possible in the table for each one. Everything will become clear by the end of the chapter.

SITUATION	My child doesn't know how to tie their own shoelaces.
OPPORTUNITY	Every time we leave the house
KNOWLEDGE	How to tie shoelaces
ABILITY	The ability to tie knots and bows
MOTIVATION	Become more independent

▼ 16%

🕐 8 mins

Personal Responsibility

Child's personal responsibilities:
- their toys, clothes, schoolbag and books
- personal hygiene and grooming, brushing teeth, getting dressed, their own body
- their bedroom and personal space
- homework and extracurricular activities

❯ **Write down which of these responsibilities you take on for your child.**

_____

_____

_____

_____

_____

❯ **In which areas would you like to increase your child's level of personal responsibility from now on?**

_____

_____

_____

_____

_____

▼ 19%

🕐 3 mins

General Responsibility

> **General responsibilities:**
> - general housekeeping rules
> **Civic duty:**
> - taking care of the environment
> - good manners

❯ **What housekeeping tasks would you like your child to do? Write them below.**
e.g. Changing the toilet roll, putting laundered clothes back in the wardrobe

_____

_____

❯ **What civic responsibilities would you like your child to take on? Write them below.**
e.g. Holding onto rubbish until they find a bin

_____

_____

▼ 23%

🕐 6 mins 📖 p. 254

Specific Responsibility

Specific responsibilities
- your child's specific chores
- school and homework

❯ **Make a list of the chores you could give your child. Be as specific as you can.**

_____

_____

_____

_____

_____

_____

▼ 26%

> **Choose one of those chores and discuss it with your child today. Ask them how and when they think they're going to do it. Encourage them to be as specific as possible. Put your promises into action.**
> **e.g.** They will water the plants after lunch on Tuesdays, Thursdays and Saturdays.

⏱ 10 mins 📖 p. 255

Personal Responsibility — Examples

1. Responsibility over your own body

Techniques:
1. 'It's freezing outside. You might be cold.'
2. 'What could you do so that you're not cold?'
3. 'It's your body, you decide. You're the best person to take care of it.'

❯ Think of a situation related to your child's body.
Using an example from today's episode, write down a few questions you could ask them. Make them aware of their body and the responsibility they have over it.

_____

_____

_____

_____

2. Responsibility for personal things
❯ Imagine you're going out to the park. Use the techniques you've learnt today and give an answer to each toy-related situation.

• 'I want to take all my toys with me!' (points towards a mountain of toys)

• 'You hold them, my hands hurt!'

▼ 32%

- You arrive at the park. What do you do with the toys now?

- What do you do when you leave the park?

> **Come up with a set of rules for cleaning your child's bedroom. What is the minimum that you expect every day? What needs doing once a week or once a month?**
> **Write these rules below. Throughout the course of this chapter, find out how to communicate these rules effectively.**

Your rules about your child's room

Every day

Weekly

Monthly

▼ 35%

🕐 9 mins

Competence, Step by Step

❯ Which skills would you like your child to have?
Choose one of them and write it below. You can repeat this process on one of the blank pages at the end of the chapter.
e.g. Being able to dress themselves

1 **Break the learning process down into small steps.** Write those steps below. **e.g.** 1. put on pants and socks 2. put on a top, etc.

2 **Plan time** when you can put these steps into practice.
First show them what to do, then do it together.

3 **Give praise for effort and praise their progress.** Soon they'll have ownership of the new task. Stay with them throughout the whole process. Write down how long it took them to do each step alone (but not necessarily perfectly).

4 **Mastering tasks and acquiring competence.** 'Sooner or later, you'll know how to do this as well as a grown-up.'

▼ 39%

🕐 4 mins

Change the Environment so That They Can Do It on Their Own

❯ Using what you've learnt in this episode, write down the things your child could do.

_____   _____
_____   _____
_____   _____
_____   _____
_____   _____
_____   _____
_____   _____
_____   _____
_____   _____

❯ How could you change the environment at home and re-arrange furniture or other items so that your child can do more things by themselves?

_____
_____
_____
_____
_____
_____
_____
_____

▼ 42%

🕑 6 mins

The World Is Full of Resources, Teach Children How to Use Them

▶ What kind of resources do you have in the house that you could use when your child asks you something?

_____   _____

_____   _____

_____   _____

▶ Think about your family members. Maybe some of them are experts or enthusiasts in certain fields. Write them down below and then encourage your child to call upon these family members when they have a question.

Name: Knows a lot about:

_____   _____

_____   _____

_____   _____

_____   _____

▼ 45%

🕐 5 mins

They Ask You 'Why' Questions? Ask Them Back

 Focus on learning. Show your child that it's fun and useful to learn and find out about new things.

❯ **Write a list of replies that you could give your child when they ask 'why?'.**
Now you always have them at hand and they'll be easy to use.

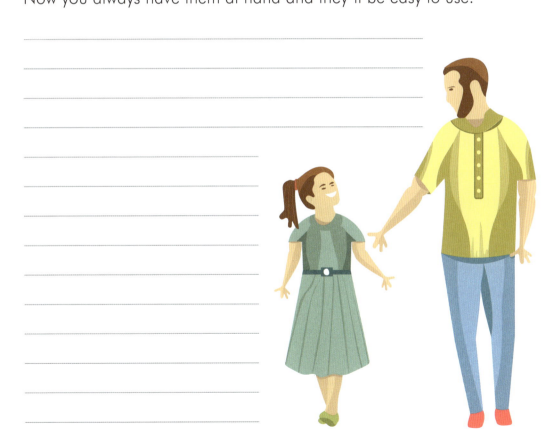

▼ 48%

Encourage Without Forcing

> Find the reasons why your child gives up on various things. Is it their fault they **can't**? Do they feel like they're not **capable**? Do they throw in the towel because they just **don't want to**?
>
> Whenever your child wants to quit something, come back to this episode, look at these exercises and try to find the **cause** of them giving up.

▼ 52%

🕐 6 mins

Ask for Permission to Help

❯ When your child can't do something, what do you say?
Fill in the sentences below with the keyword.

'You can't do that _____.'
'You're not big enough _____ to be able to reach that.
Next year you'll be able to.'

❯ Ask for permission every time you want to help.
Write down the sentences that you've learnt today for doing this.
Don't forget, this is how you fulfil your child's Need for Competence
and Need for Autonomy.

▼ 55%

🕐 5 mins

It's not Easy, It's Hard! Recognise That

❯ Write down some activities where your child gets frustrated or gives up easily because it's difficult.
e.g. 500-piece jigsaw puzzles, maths homework, etc.

_____

_____

_____

❯ What could you say to them to give them encouragement? Use the information you received today and write a few replies.

_____

_____

_____

_____

_____

_____

_____

❯ You're going to be taking your child to do something unpleasant but necessary. How do you tell them about it?
e.g. You're going to the doctor's for a procedure that you know will be painful.

_____

_____

_____

▼ 58%

🕐 7 mins

Give Balanced Feedback

❯ Write down some examples of negative feedback.
e.g. 'You still have 4 toys on the floor.'

_____

_____

❯ Write down some of the reasons why this is not beneficial and doesn't speed up the learning process.

_____

_____

_____

❯ Write down some examples of positive feedback.
e.g. 'Well done!', 'You're the best', 'Fantastic!'

_____

_____

_____

❯ Write down an example of a compliment sandwich, so you have another way of saying 'not like that'.

_____

_____

_____

_____

▼ 61%

🕐 7 mins

Balanced Feedback — Examples

STEP 1	**STEP 2**	**STEP 3**
Highlight the **pluses.** Describe them.	Highlight the **minuses.** Describe them.	Finish with some **encouragement.**

Tip: Take a breath between steps 1 and 2.
Yes: 'You've dressed yourself and put your trousers and T-shirt on right. Yay! Now let's have a look at these socks. I think you might have them inside out. I know you're going to be able to put them back on the right way.' **No**: 'You've put your T-shirt on right but your socks are inside out.'

❯ Think of a few situations in which your child has only done part of a task or only partly improved a behaviour.
Offer them balanced feedback using the structure shown in today's episode.
e.g. They have started cleaning their bedroom but haven't finished.
They have prepared lunch but haven't washed the dishes.
They wanted to learn something new, but it didn't turn out well at all.

_____

_____

_____

_____

 64%

8 mins

Thinking out Loud — Examples

 There is a process behind every decision. Think out loud to develop your child's ability to make decisions, think critically and become competent. **Talk your child through the things you are doing, step by step.**

❯ **What strengths could you teach your child by thinking out loud?**
Write them below. Jot down a few situations in your day-to-day life that exemplify these skills, thinking out loud.

_____

_____

_____

_____

❯ **What are your partner's strengths? What do their grandparents, family and friends know how to do well?**
Write these abilities below and ask each of these people to apply this technique with you. You'll raise an extremely competent child.

_____

_____

_____

_____

_____

▼ 68%

🕐 7 mins

Be a Role Model

❯ Write down 5 behaviours, skills or traits that you would like to develop in your child.

_____

_____

_____

_____

_____

❯ Write down the replies and gestures you could use — as theatrically and obviously as you can — to demonstrate this behaviour every time you get the chance.

_____

_____

_____

_____

_____

_____

_____

_____

_____

_____

▼ 71%

🕐 5 mins

Respect Their Personal Space and Privacy

❯ Write down some rules that you could set at home to ensure that each family member's personal space and privacy are respected. You can use examples from today's episode.

▼ 74%

🕐 4 mins

Avoid Using 'We'

❯ **What are the situations in which you use 'We' when responsibility for that action actually lies solely with your child?**
Write them down. Make a conscious decision that from now on, you are not going to do that anymore.

_____

_____

_____

_____

_____

_____

_____

_____

_____

▼ 77%

🕐 7 mins

Encourage Them in the Areas Where They Are Most Competent

❯ **What are your child's talents?**
Write down at least 3 talents.
e.g. They sing really well.

_____

_____

_____

❯**What are the areas where you would like your child to improve?**
e.g. I'd like them to wash the dishes after dinner.

_____

_____

_____

❯**How could you combine the 2 to reach your objective?**
e.g. They can sing and listen to loud music (agree on a maximum volume) when it's their turn to wash the dishes after dinner.

_____

_____

_____

_____

_____

▼ 80%

🕐 7 mins

Mistakes Are Learning Opportunities

1 'What can you do next time so that _____?'

2 Explain the process, procedure or rules to them.

3 Make sure they have understood. Ask them to repeat everything back.

4 Give them the opportunity to demonstrate that they have understood. Before that happens, open up the discussion again.

❯ Think of a recent mistake that your child has made.
How could you have reacted, without punishing or raising your voice, to speed up the learning process and let them know what to do next time? Write this conversation below.

_____

_____

_____

_____

_____

_____

_____

_____

_____

▼ 84%

6 mins

Allow Natural Consequences to Occur

 Criteria for allowing natural consequences to happen:
1. It must be **safe** — your child must not be in danger.
2. It must be **immediate** — the consequence must occur very quickly.
3. It must be **visible**, palpable and definite — the consequence must be obvious.

❯ Write down 3 examples of situations where you prevent your child from testing out the natural consequences of their actions.

_____

_____

_____

❯ What would happen if you didn't step in?

_____

_____

_____

_____

 Underline the safe, immediate and obvious consequences. Could you let them happen? Try to do so. Your child might learn more the hard way.

▼ 87%

Score: /10

What Have You Learnt so Far?

Congratulations!
You've completed **Chapter 4**.

Take this self-evaluation test to see how well you've taken on board the information we've shared with you. Depending on the results, you'll see whether what you've learnt has sunk in or whether you need to watch some episodes again. Check your answers at the end of the Playbook.

 If you'd like to know your result immediately without having to add up scores, you can take the test **online**. Go to **https://bit.ly/TestChapter4** or scan the QR code.

1. What are the consequences when parents do things for their children?
a. The child will learn the value of work and copy their parent's example.
b. The child will not develop that particular ability. They won't fulfil the Need for Competence either.
c. They fulfil the Need for Relatedness and the child feels loved and understood.

2. How do you increase a child's competence? Choose the true statements in the list below.
a. Do things for them as often as possible so that they see how to do them properly and follow your example.
b. Answer 'Why?' with another question to keep their thirst for knowledge alive.

▼ 90%

c. Raise standards as high as possible. If you don't aim high, they won't reach the top.

d. Change the environment so that your child can do certain activities by themselves.

e. Give them total freedom so that they can learn to be self-reliant.

f. Plan in advance which skill you want to teach and take the time to do it.

g. Encourage them to look for and find answers to their questions from various sources.

h. Tell them the truth about the difficulty of the activity they're about to try so that they're prepared for the extra effort and possible failure.

3. **Which of these parenting styles matches the statement below, in relation to competence and responsibility?**
Write the appropriate letter in the box on the left. **A** for Authoritarian, **P** for Permissive and **B** for Balanced.

a. Makes decisions for their child. The child has no say in the matter.

b. 'It's your body, you're the best person to take care of it.'

c. Offers more freedom than the child can handle.

d. Encourages the child to do an activity, without forcing them.

e. The child's aptitude is greater than the freedom their parent gives them.

f. Encourages and congratulates their child, regardless of the results.

g. When the child wants to give up, they force them to continue at any cost.

h. Will give their child freedom after they have demonstrated the necessary aptitude.

i. Addresses the child in the singular so as not to diminish responsibility.

▼ 93%

4. Fill in the triangle of competence with the appropriate verbs.

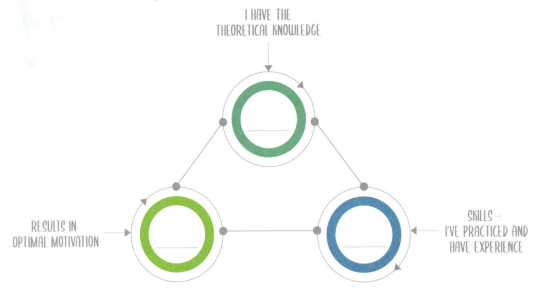

I HAVE THE
THEORETICAL KNOWLEDGE

RESULTS IN
OPTIMAL MOTIVATION

SKILLS –
I'VE PRACTICED AND
HAVE EXPERIENCE

5. How do you increase your child's level of personal responsibility?

a. Make sure they are properly dressed every time they leave the house and maybe even call to check if they're cold or have had enough to eat.

b. Explain to them what will happen if they don't listen; in the end, they will understand and will do as they're told.

c. Explain to them that they are the best person to take care of their own body and personal belongings, set rules.

6. How do you increase your child's level of general responsibility?

a. Do housework together and explain each stage to them.

b. They will become responsible when they're older. Until then, I'll do everything for them.

c. Stand over them until they've done everything you told them to do.

97% ▼

7. What are the consequences of giving a child responsibility for a specific task?

a. They will feel used. Children shouldn't be 'put to work'.

b. They're too young for household chores, they'll definitely break something.

c. It prepares them, as a future adult, for the interdependent relationships they will have with other adults and the responsibility they have for their own space.

8. What do you do when a child wants to give up an activity?

a. Encourage them to continue because you've paid money for that activity.

b. Don't force them to do anything. They'll float from one activity to another. It's good to do a bit of everything.

c. Firstly, find out the reason. Unless they're categoric about it, assure them that although it's hard now, in the future it will actually be fun.

9. What happens when you tell a child that an activity is easy when it's hard?

a. You encourage them. If you told them it was hard, they wouldn't want to try.

b. They'll realise that actually it's not all that hard.

c. They will get discouraged if they don't succeed the first time and they won't feel capable, even if they can do it; their Need for Competence will suffer.

10. Choose the most appropriate feedback from the options below.

a. 'Great job! Congratulations! What you did was really good! We are proud of you!'

b. 'I see you finished all your homework before I came home from work. That's really good. Finish putting away the clothes on your bed and then you'll have the whole evening free. I know you can do that quickly.'

c. 'I'm glad you did your homework, that's really good. But your room is messy. Finish tidying it and then you're done.'

100% ▾

Notes

> Jot down any other ideas or notes you want to remember from this chapter here.

Chapter 4: A Competent Child Is a Responsible Child

Notes

5

TOP METHODS FOR
GETTING KIDS TO COOPERATE

Chapter 5 Contents

Top Methods for Getting Kids to Cooperate

4 mins

Chapter 5 Introduction

01 You're going to learn **the difference between cooperation and obedience.**

02 What to avoid if you want your children to **cooperate.**

03 **Techniques:** What to say and do in various situations.

▼ 3%

🕐 11 mins | 10 mins

What NOT to Do

❯ Fill in the names of the 7 most common mistakes that you learnt in today's episode. Use the examples as a guide.

1.

'If you eat everything up, you can watch cartoons.'

2.

'If you don't come with me now, I'll leave you here!'

3.

'Well, whatever. Have another 10 minutes on the tablet.'

4.

'I can't buy you sweets now. We'll get some next time.'

5.

When your child doesn't want to leave the park, you just pick them up and carry them home.

6.

'That's not appropriate. It's just not nice.'

7.

'All right, I'll get you a toy. Just be quiet!'

▼ 6%

❯ Choose the 5 most common 'refusal' behaviours your child displays.
Next to them, write how you react to them.
Which reactions from the 'What not to do' list have you had?

Your child's refusals	Reactions from the 'What not to do' list

▼ 9%

The 3 Basic Psychological Needs in the Context of Cooperation

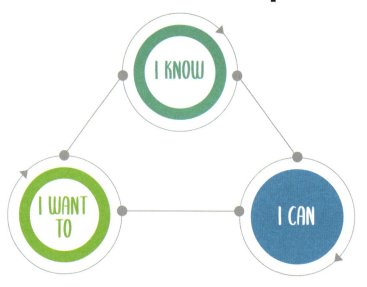

❯ Write down the objectives for this chapter (the ones you learnt about in the episode).

▼ 11%

🕐 7 mins

4 Reasons That Make Us Unhappy

❯ According to the William Glasser Institute, what are the 4 reasons for unhappiness that stem from an exacerbated Need for Autonomy?

_____

_____

_____

_____

❯ Below, write down any behaviour that bothers you in the people in your household. In the right-hand column, write down what you've done to convince them to change this behaviour.

Annoying behaviour	Actions

❯ Which of these behaviours do you think you could accept? Which of them do you think are reasonable to live with? Highlight and remember them.

How to Set Rules and Boundaries

❯ **What are the areas of conflict in your family?**
What situations arise daily that you have not been able to find a solution to? Write them below.

Area of conflict	Rule: What do you expect to happen?	When?	How?
Your child just throws their coat and shoes on the floor when they walk into the house	Coats, hats and shoes should be put away in the right place	When you come home you must immediately take your outdoor clothes off	Coat on the hook, hats and gloves on the shelf, shoes on the shoe rack

▼ 17%

For each of these situations, set one rule or limit.
Expand: What do you expect to happen? When? How? Under what conditions?

Under what conditions?	Exceptions	Consequences for breaking the rules
In the hall, before coming into the house	When we come home late in the evening and you're very tired	You will get your dinner after you've put your clothes in the right place

▼ 20%

🕐 5 mins

Follow the Rules for Setting Rules

❯ Which adults make the rules? Who will you sit down with to discuss and take stock? Write their name below.

_____

_____

_____

❯ When do you plan on having this discussion? Set a day.
Write it in your diary.

 Please use the tables in the back of the Playbook. You can photocopy them or download the list in the size you want. I encourage you to fill them out together with your child.

▼ 23%

Use Visual Aids

❯ For which of the rules that you've set could you use visual aids? Choose 2 of them and draw them below.

At the back of the Playbook, you will also find a poster that will help you make all these rules into a visual. Why not fill it out with your child?

26%

Establish and Follow Routines

❯ Write down times when there are arguments in your family.
e.g. In the morning before school

_____   _____

_____   _____

_____   _____

_____   _____

❯ What routines could you set up for those times to make it easier for everybody?
Write the steps below then, with your child, transcribe them onto the poster at the back of the Playbook.

7 mins

Use Empathy

❯ Make a list of the situations where your child wants something or is crying and you tend to respond with a lack of empathy.

_____

_____

❯ Now that you know how much empathy helps, write down some replies below that you can use so your child feels understood and is more receptive to what you say.

_____

_____

_____

_____

_____

_____

▼ 31%

🕐 6 mins 📖 p. 260

Prepping Ahead of Time

❯ Select 2 situations in which your child gets impatient or agitated. What could you do beforehand to prevent bad reactions?

Scenario: ....
Plan:

Scenario: ....
Plan:

▼ 34%

❯ Think of an upcoming event in your family. It may be a family trip or a visit to the dentist.
Write down everything you know will happen at this event.

❯ Jot down your expectations about your child's behaviour.

 After you've written them down, tell your child about them. Do this every time you have a new activity. Your child will be more willing to cooperate.

🕐 5 mins

Tell Your Child What to Do

> Make a list of negative pressures that you communicate to your child or partner. Reformulate them.

Negative pressures	Reformulate

▼ 40%

Episode 16

🕐 4 mins

Use Code Words

❯ What are the nagging phrases that you use on your child daily? What code word could you use to remind your child what they've done without nagging?

Unpleasant situation	Code word
e.g. 'Don't slouch! Stand up straight!'	'Back'

▼ 43%

🕐 4 mins

Highlight the Traits You Want to See in Them

 Every time that your child does something good, name that quality and describe its benefits.

❯ Jot down the things that you would like your child to do. What qualities are they demonstrating with these actions? What benefits do these qualities have?

Activities	Quality	Benefits of the quality
sharing toys	generosity	when you share things, it makes people happy

▼ 46%

🕐 5 mins

Offer an Alternative

❯ **Things are forbidden, but your child still does them?**
How could you reformulate the rule to offer an alternative?

e.g. Your small child wants to climb the stairs by themselves.
Instead of: 'Don't climb the stairs!'
Offer the alternative: 'You can climb the stairs if I'm standing next to you.'

_____

_____

_____

_____

▼ 48%

🕐 3 mins

Put Conditions on 'Yes'

❯ **Which of your child's wants could you put conditions on?**
Write down the conditions using 'if', 'how', 'where', 'under what conditions'.

e.g. Your child wants to watch cartoons, but you're getting ready to go out.
Instead of: 'You can't watch cartoons. We haven't got time for cartoons.'
Condition: 'You can only watch something if you agree to turn off the TV after I've finished getting your brother dressed.'

_____

_____

_____

_____

_____

▼ 51%

🕐 4 mins

Replace IF With AFTER

❯ Think of the sequences in certain actions.
Write down responses that you could give your child using 'after'.

e.g. 'You can go out **after** you've finished your homework.'

▼ 54%

🕐 5 mins

Make Your Boundaries Clear

❯ **Write down the areas where your child is the most undecided.**
e.g. They can never decide which clothes they want to buy when shopping.

_____

_____

_____

_____

_____

❯ **What limits could you set in these situations?**
Write them down, then communicate them at the appropriate time.

e.g. 'I have 2 hours for shopping. At the end of that time, you need to have chosen all the things you need. We can only buy them if you've picked out the ones you want. And once you've chosen them, we won't be exchanging them.'

_____

_____

_____

_____

_____

_____

❝ Help them to decide. Don't forget to emphasise the importance of making a decision and sticking to it, and the consequences of that decision.

▼ 57%

🕐 4 mins

Ask Your Child About Consequences

❯ Jot down some of the wishes your child tells you about most often or persistently.

e.g. Your teenager wants to go on a road trip.

❯ What might be the consequences?
After you've written them down, talk to your child about them so that they can come to the same conclusions.

e.g. Your teenager wants to go on a road trip. They are the only one of their friends with a driving licence. They won't be able to take a break from driving, it will all be on their shoulders. If they're not feeling well, there will be nobody to take over.

▼ 60%

🕐 3 mins

Ask for Time to Think

❯ Write a list of your child's requests where you could ask for thinking time before answering.

e.g. 'Mum, will you buy me a phone?'
'Give me some time to think about it and discuss it with your dad. We'll tell you what we decide in a couple of days.'

_____

_____

_____

_____

_____

_____

_____

_____

_____

_____

_____

_____

_____

▼ 63%

🕐 3 mins

Let Their Imagination Flow

❯ What things does your child want that you can't let them or don't want them to have? Firstly, empathise with what they want. Then write down what questions you could ask to fulfil their desire for imagination.

> **e.g.** 'Would you like us to have a cat at home? What would you call it? What colour would it be? Where would it sleep? Who'd feed it? Who'd wake up early in the morning to let it out?'

▼ 66%

🕐 5 mins

Use Humour

❯ Observe your partner or another person in your life. What humour do they use to make your child laugh so that they cooperate more easily? Below, make a list of those funny responses.

Remember these 'techniques' and use them yourself with your child. Parenting will become more fun for you too.

_____

_____

_____

_____

_____

_____

_____

_____

_____

_____

_____

_____

▼ 68%

Reinforce Their Responsibilities

❯ Look at the exercises you did in Chapter 4 related to responsibility. Write down a final list of chores to increase their level of responsibility across the 3 areas.
What would you keep from the old list? What would you add?

Personal belongings, their bedroom, their responsibilities

▼ 71%

Their body

Choices and decisions

▼ 74%

4 mins

Do Your Job With a Smile

❯ **Which chores do you enjoy? How can you tell?**
e.g. I dance while vacuuming.

_____

_____

_____

_____

❯ **Which of your daily chores do you like the least?**
e.g. Cooking

_____

_____

_____

_____

❯ **How can you transform these 'unpleasant' chores so that they are more pleasurable, or at least seem so to your child?**
e.g. I could put music on in the kitchen and dance while I make dinner.

_____

_____

_____

_____

▼ 77%

Involve Your Child in What You're Doing

❯ Which 'real-life' activities could you involve your child in? Remember the benefits of involving them. This is how you find yourself becoming more patient.
e.g. Going to the bank, shopping, looking for a gift

▼ 80%

🕐 5 mins | 6 mins | 10 mins

Give Options Within Limits

Authoritarian Parenting
'Please sit down at the table and eat your dinner.'

Permissive Parenting
'What do you want? Soup or sandwiches?' or 'Won't you eat something? I'll make you whatever you want.'

Balanced Parenting
'I would like you to eat some healthy food' — this is the limit you set. 'Do you want soup or chicken? It's your choice.'

STEP 1	STEP 2	STEP 3
Give them the limit, state your request and tell them the principle or behaviour	Offer 2-3 variants	'You choose'/'You decide'/'It's your choice'

(that you want your child to demonstrate)

▼ 83%

❯ Make a list of 5 requests. Formulate them using the aforementioned steps.

❯ In what other situations could you offer your child options? Write down at least 3.

▼ 87%

Score: /12

What Have You Learnt so Far?

Congratulations!

You've completed **Chapter 5**.

Take this self-evaluation test to see how well you've taken on board the information we've shared with you. Depending on the results, you'll see whether what you've learnt has sunk in or whether you need to watch some episodes again. Check your answers at the end of the Playbook.

 If you'd like to know your result immediately without having to add up scores, you can take the test **online**. Go to **https://bit.ly/TestChapter5** or scan the QR code.

1. You're in the supermarket and your child wants a toy that you have no intention of buying them. You answer: 'I haven't got the money. I'll get it when I'm paid.' What are the long-term consequences of this type of reply?

a. Your child understands that they need to work to have money for things.

b. Your child will lose faith in you.

c. They will be impatiently awaiting payday.

2. Your child has watched enough TV. It's time to turn it off. You tell them, but you are ignored. What do you do? Choose the answer that matches a Balanced Parenting Style, according to the methods shown in this chapter.

a. Raise your voice until you're heard.

b. 'Earth to Zach! I said, turn off the TV!'

c. Sigh, but ignore them. They'll turn the TV off by themselves later. You don't want to argue with them.

▼ 91%

d. You warned them earlier: 'In 5 minutes, the TV needs to be switched off. You switch it off, or I will. You choose.'

e. You tell them once. If they don't listen, you switch off the TV and that's that.

f. After the 5-minute warning is up, you tell them the TV needs to be turned off. If they don't turn it off, you'll do it.

g. Your child needs to listen from the start. If they don't listen, turn the TV off and punish them.

3. How do you set rules or limits for your child?

a. Discuss it with your partner, grandparents and other adults involved in raising your child. Come up with a clear set of rules and involve your child in this discussion.

b. All rules are discussed amongst adults. Once the rules have been set, tell your child about the upcoming changes.

c. Your child needs to decide. Discuss it with them and negotiate limits. Make it so they are as comfortable as possible.

4. What are routines for?

a. They restrict children and don't encourage creativity. Routines don't do any good.

b. They should be as strict as possible. All families need to follow daily routines.

c. They teach your child about consequences. Children are more willing to cooperate because they know what to expect.

5. You tell your child to do their homework, but they say they don't feel like it. How do you react?

a. 'I understand you don't always feel like doing your homework. I'm sure

94% ▾

you'd much rather play. I'm sure you'd feel much more relaxed playing if you knew that your homework was done, though.'

b. 'Okay, you don't feel like it. You can play first but you'll do your homework after, right?'

c. 'No such thing as "I don't feel like it". You have to do your homework and that's what you're going to do.'

6. **Your child is crying because they wanted a toy that you don't want to (or can't) buy them. How do you respond?**

a. Children need to be happy and you also want to avoid an embarrassing scene in the shop. You buy the toy with your credit card.

b. 'I can't buy that toy now. I promise you Father Christmas will bring it.'

c. Empathise with them. Let them tell you about the toy and show them you're interested in it.

7. **How can you prevent a tantrum in the supermarket?**
a. Make sure you take enough money with you and prepare yourself mentally for them to ask.
b. You only take them shopping once they're old enough to control their emotions.
c. Make sure they've had something to eat and drink. Expect that they might ask for things and find solutions to these problems before you leave the house. Tell them you're only buying what's on the shopping list.

8. **Choose the appropriate expression for a Balanced Parent.**
a. 'Sit down at the table right now!'
b. 'Watch your step!'
c. 'Before we leave for Grandma's, your toys need to be put away.'
d. 'You'll put your coat on, won't you?'

97% ▼

e. 'No touching the plugs!'

f. 'I don't know if I'll buy you a phone. Give me until Monday to think about it.'

9. **How do you correctly add conditions when fulfilling a want?**

a. 'I'll give you dessert, if you clear your plate away.'

b. 'Yes, you can go to the party, if you agree to be back by 10 o'clock.'

c. 'I'll give you the car once you've demonstrated you can be responsible.'

10. **What do you do when your child changes their mind?**

a. I give them what they need. At the end of the day, if they change their mind, it means they don't like it. You can't force a child to do something they don't like.

b. They get nothing. Take away their first choice and don't give them their second. That's how they'll learn not to keep changing their mind.

c. I give them the limits beforehand and tell them that once they've made the decision, I won't be around to make changes.

11. **Your child wants to invite all their classmates to their birthday party, which you are holding in your flat. How do you react?**

a. 'Where are we going to fit these 30 children? It's a bit much, don't you think?'

b. You know that it won't be comfortable but you do what they want. You want them to learn from their mistakes and experience the consequences for themselves.

c. You ask them in a way that makes them realise by themselves what the scenario would look like and come to the appropriate conclusion.

12. **Your child climbs onto the table. How do you react?**

a. Take the plates off the table and leave them in peace. They need to explore. You mustn't limit the Need for Competence.

b. 'Don't climb on the table. You'll fall!' If they don't listen, grab them by the arm and pull them down.

c. Explain to them that if they climb on the table, they may fall and hurt themselves. If it's OK with you, you can let them do this so they explore the consequences of their own actions.

100% ▾

Jot down any other ideas or notes you want to remember from this chapter here.

Notes

Chapter 5: Top Methods for Getting Kids to Cooperate

Notes

Chapter 5: Top Methods for Getting Kids to Cooperate

6

SOLVING PROBLEMS AND MAKING DECISIONS

Chapter 6 Contents

Solving Problems and Making Decisions

Chapter 6 Introduction

You're going to learn the difference between your child's problems and your own.

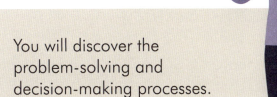

You will discover the problem-solving and decision-making processes.

▼ 2%

🕐 3 mins

6 Skills to Be Successful

The Science Behind Making Decisions and Solving Problems

Self-Discipline

6 SKILLS THAT LEAD US TO BE HAPPY AND SUCCESSFUL IN LIFE

Self-Esteem

Managing Emotions

Social Skills

Controlling Impulses

❯ In order to raise a happy child, we need to develop all of these skills. To start, write down which of the 6 you believe are your strengths, where you still need a little work and where you consider you still have a long way to go. It will put your progress into perspective.

▼ 5%

Episode 2

📖 P. 261

Strengths

Areas for improvement

Skills to develop

▼ 7%

🕐 5 mins

How We Solve 'Adult' Problems

❯ Think back to a situation where a friend came to you to share a problem. How did you react? How did you speak to them? What did you say?

_____

_____

_____

_____

❯ Which of these behaviours would you like to repeat in a similar situation with your child?

_____

_____

_____

❯ Which would you not want to repeat?

_____

_____

_____

❯ Imagine that you are in a difficult situation. You can't see any way out, so you call a friend.
What do you need them to do?

▼ 10%

> How do they speak to you?

> What do they say?

> What is your real need in that moment?

🕐 3 mins

What Not to Do:
Show Impatience or Disinterest

➤ Unconsciously, this is what we are telling our children when we don't pay them proper attention or are impatient.

'I don't know the right words yet to explain everything that's happening, that's why I babble. I can see that you're already losing patience. It must mean my problem is not very important to you. I'm not worthwhile enough for daddy to listen to me.'

▼ 15%

❯ In the next 2 days, tell yourself that you're going to pay attention to your reactions when your child comes to you with a problem. Each time, jot down:

What you did when they told you their problem	What the problem they brought to you was	How you reacted

▼ 17%

⟳ 2 mins

What Not to Do: Give Advice, Solutions or Lectures

❯ Think back to and write down the last problem your child came to you with, big or small.

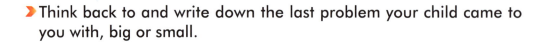

❯ How did you react?

❯ What advice did you give?

❯ How did your child react to the advice you gave?

❯ Did they apply the tips, solutions and lecturing you gave them? Did this solve the problem?

Tell yourself that from now on, you are going to stop offering these kinds of 'solutions'. You'll soon start seeing an improvement in your relationship.

▼ 19%

2 mins

What Not to Do: Blame, Judge or Threaten

❯ Below, write about a time when you told your parents about a problem and they reacted in one of the following ways: blame, judgement or threats.

❯ What were the exact words that your parents used in that situation? **e.g.** 'See what happens if you're lazy? Any more grades like that and you can say goodbye to the computer.' 'You're just coasting.'

❯ How did you feel?

❯ What impact do you think those words had on how you are now as an adult?

❯ Write down a promise not to judge, threaten or make your child feel guilty when they ask for help with a problem.

🕐 5 mins

What Not to Do: Distract or Dismiss Their Feelings

❯ Think back to when your parents reacted this way to your problems. Write out the situation below.

_____

_____

_____

_____

_____

_____

_____

_____

❯ Which of these reactions has become a way of behaving for you? Write down 2 situations where you have minimised problems to distract your child's attention. Promise yourself that you're not going to do this anymore.

_____

_____

_____

_____

_____

_____

_____

▼ 24%

🕐 7 mins

What Are Children's Problems?

❱ Write down the problems that your child has faced in the last 3 months in these 3 categories.

1. Relationships with other children

2. School and extracurricular activities

3. Handling emotions

▼ 27%

🕐 6 mins

What Are Adults' Problems?

❯ For each category, write down 3 examples of problems that you had to solve in your capacity as a parent.

1. Problems related to property
e.g. Your child broke a window at school.

2. Beliefs, principles and societal norms
e.g. How they wanted to dress for various occasions (funeral, wedding, trips, etc.)

3. Health and safety
e.g. Medical treatment

4. Education
e.g. Which nursery school they'll go to

5. Household rules
e.g. Screen time

▼ 29%

8 mins

The Definition of 'Problem'

> Problems are the difference between what we expect and reality. We don't know the cause of these differences.

❯ **Fill in the 3 key questions you need to ask to see whether a situation you are facing requires problem-solving or decision-making.**

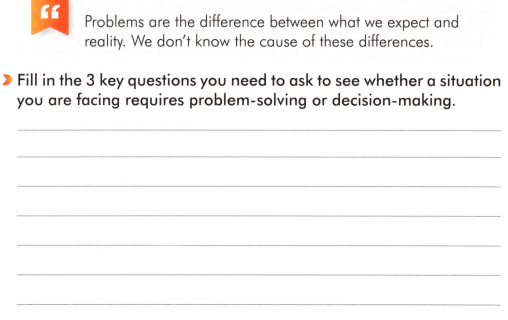

If you answered 'yes' to all these questions, start by looking into the true cause of the problem.

> If you want to solve a problem, you first need to know its cause.

❯ **Complete the sentences below with the keywords: past/future.**

Problem refers to the _____, decision refers to _____.

▼ 32%

Episode 13

 4 mins

The Definition of 'Decision'

> Decisions are situations in which we have to choose between 2 or more options. It's about reaching an objective.

▶ Write down the 3 biggest concerns you have at the moment. Put a **yes** or **no** in the columns with questions. You'll see which of them are problems where you need to make a decision and which are just thoughts.

Your concern	Any differences between expectation and reality?	Know the causes of these differences?	Need to know causes to resolve problem?

🕐 4 mins

The 4 'S's

❯ Below, write down a few words or a short sentence that explain each of the 'S's when it comes to problem-solving, as we saw in today's episode.

1. Sentiment

_____

_____

_____

2. Situation

_____

_____

_____

3. Solutions

_____

_____

_____

4. Success

_____

_____

_____

▼ 36%

🕐 4 mins

Ask Questions About Their Feelings

❯ Think back to a problematic situation you have often had with your child. What beliefs usually lie behind their feelings?
Below, write one or more questions you could ask them to explore these beliefs.

e.g. 'Talk to me a bit about why you think the other person doesn't like you.'
'Can you explain to me why you think these girls are ignoring you?'

BRING FEELINGS OUT INTO THE OPEN

Sentiments

Stressful
situations

▼ 39%

🕐 4 mins

Confirm You Understand Without Judging

What to remember: Don't judge other people's feelings and perceptions. Paraphrase and repeat back what your child says to you.

❯ Apply what you learnt in this episode — ask questions and answer in an empathetic way.

1. 'Oh mum! Rob's dumped me! He says he likes someone else more than me!'

_____

_____

_____

_____

2. 'The teacher made me sit on the naughty chair in school. All the others were laughing at me!'

_____

_____

_____

_____

3. 'Nobody wanted to play with me today. They said I was stupid and they don't play with stupid people. I never want to go to school again!'

_____

_____

_____

_____

▼ 41%

Put Their Feelings Into Words

> The first step in managing emotions is being able to know what emotion or sentiment you're feeling.

▶ **Think about some highly emotional situations your child often finds themselves in.**
What feelings do they express? Write these feelings below, one column for positive, the other for negative.
The next time they're in a similar situation, tell them how they're feeling. Fill in the lists every time you notice a new emotion.

Positive emotions	Negative emotions

▼ 44%

🕐 3 mins

Talk About Your Feelings

❯ Enrich your vocabulary with words that define your feelings. Write down the 2 most common feelings you have most days and the situations that trigger them. Then write down how you could tell your child about what you're feeling.

Feeling:

upset

Scenario: Your child is sick and in pain
How do you talk about feelings with your child?
'I know your tummy hurts. I am sad too when I see you like this and I know that I can't do much to make you feel better.'

Feeling:

Scenario: _____
How do you talk about feelings with your child?

Feeling:

Scenario: _____
How do you talk about feelings with your child?

▼ 46%

🕐 5 mins

Highlight Emotions of Fictional Characters

" Talk about the emotions, feelings, intentions and beliefs of the characters in storybooks or cartoons to develop your child's sense of empathy.

❯ What's your child's favourite storybook?

_____

❯ Which of the character's feelings could you highlight next time you read that story? Write them below.

_____

_____

_____

_____

_____

_____

_____

_____

_____

_____

▼ 49%

Avoid Repeating Labels

 Be sure to differentiate between labels that define behaviour and specific outbursts of behaviour. Never use unkind nicknames for your child.

> **What labels did others put on you in your childhood that influenced your development?**

_____

_____

> **What labels are you putting on your child?**

_____

_____

> **What labels do other people put on your child?**

_____

_____

Make the conscious decision that you're no longer going to use these names.

▼ 51%

⏱ 2 mins

It's not 'Us', It's 'You'

What to remember: If the problem that needs solving is your child's problem, address it with them directly. Send the message that 'this is your problem and I'm going to help you solve it'.

❯ Write down some questions and statements where you usually use the plural, and reformulate them using the correct pronoun.

3 mins

The Purpose of Exploring the Situation

> Think of a real or hypothetical situation where your child has a problem with another child or adult.
> Write down 5 questions you could ask your child to understand the situation better and help them to see it from more than one perspective.

▼ 56%

5 mins

Ask What It Looks Like From Other People's Point of View

 By asking your child questions, they can see the different facets of a problem for themselves and may even come up with solutions. It's important to ask them how they see the situation from the other person's point of view.

> Work on the situation from the previous episode.
Write more questions that you could ask your child so that they have a better overview of the whole situation.

_____

_____

_____

_____

_____

_____

_____

_____

_____

_____

▼ 58%

🕐 **6 mins**

Examples of Discussions About the First 2 'S's

> The purpose of the first 2 'S's — **Sentiments** and **Situation** — is to clearly state the problem and have a clear diagnosis.

❯ **Think up another scenario, either real or imaginary.**
Write down 10 questions using the model you've been learning. Be sure to check off all of the characteristics for each question.
e.g. Your child refuses to go to school or an extracurricular activity because they got told off by the teacher.

☐ open questions ☐ no judgement ☐ no advice ☐ no seeking solutions
☐ no minimising ☐ no distracting attention from the problem ☐ no threats
☐ show you've understood how they feel ☐ ask about the others involved

▼ 61%

🕐 3 mins

Confirm They Want to Solve the Problem

So far, you have learnt how to:

correctly state the problem
get an appropriate diagnosis
discover the causes of the problem

If you still don't have the answer to one or more points, do the exercises again and talk to your child before reaching a solution.

❯ **The following step is to ensure that your child actually wants to solve the problem. Write down some examples of questions as you saw in today's episode.**
e.g. 'Do you want us to find a solution together?'

▼ 63%

7 mins

Explore Options

Let your child come up with different ways of solving the problem. Continue the steps using the problem you chose in Chapter 24. Write down the questions you would ask your child so that they could find solutions together with you. Use the model below.

▶ Write down a question that will encourage them to solve the problem themselves.

_____

_____

▶ Write down a question where you provide variations on the solutions.

_____

_____

▶ Write down a question that references a similar situation in your life or theirs.

_____

_____

▶ Write down a question that will highlight the impact of their behaviour in the future.
e.g. 'How do you think the girls would feel if you said that?' 'What do you think would happen if you cheated in the test?'

_____

_____

Check with them that they want to try the solution you've arrived at together.

▼ 66%

Confirm and Practice the Solution

Check one last time that your child wants to put the solution into action.

Ask them to look at the situation from both sides of the fence so that they know what to expect when they put the suggested solution into action.

Try out your suggested solution in a role play.

▼ 68%

2 mins

The Fourth 'S' — The Purpose of This Step

 Problem-solving doesn't stop when you find a solution. It only happens once you've successfully applied that solution.

WHAT NEEDS DOING?	**WHEN WILL THEY DO IT?**
EXACTLY HOW WILL THEY DO IT?	**UNDER WHAT CONDITIONS?**

 Debrief. Once they've put the solution into practice, discuss the results, whether good or bad.

▼ 70%

Follow-Up and Examples

 How to debrief:
Be aware of their mood when they come home and adjust your tone and level of enthusiasm accordingly.
1. If they weren't successful or didn't even try, update the plan. Run through the 4'S's again in your discussion.
2. If the plan was successful, empathise with your child. Congratulate them. Find ways they could follow the same plan in other circumstances.

❯ **It's time to push this algorithm further.**
Work on the problem you chose.
Write 3 questions/statements from your debrief for both scenarios.

Your child saw the plan through successfully:

_____

_____

_____

_____

They weren't successful/didn't attempt the plan:

_____

_____

_____

_____

▼ 73%

Now take the same problem and go through the 4'S's problem-solving algorithm.

▶ What kinds of questions would you ask to bring SENTIMENTS to the surface?

_____

_____

_____

_____

▶ What kinds of questions would you ask to explore the SITUATION and find the cause?

_____

_____

_____

_____

▶ What kinds of questions would you ask to find some possible SOLUTIONS? How could you put the questions to make sure the discussion goes both ways?

_____

_____

_____

_____

▶ How will you measure SUCCESS? Once you've put the plan in place, look at the results and see what aspects of the plan you would keep and what needs adapting.

_____

_____

_____

_____

▼ 75%

⏱ 10 mins 📖 p. 263

Decision-Making in Choices and Purchases

❯ Think of a choice or a decision you will have to make in the future. Go through the 4 steps of the decision-making process. Use this page for the FIRST exercise and the next page for a different decision you'll have to make in the future.

Step 1: Objective

Step 2: Criteria

Criteria NEEDS	Criteria WANTS

Step 3: Alternatives

_____

_____

_____

_____

Step 4: **Compare the alternatives using the criteria. Write down your decision.**

▼ 78%

Step 1: Objective

Step 2: Criteria

Criteria
NEEDS

Criteria
WANTS

Step 3: Alternatives

Step 4: Compare the alternatives using the criteria. Write down your decision.

▼ 80%

An Important Core Belief

'You can find solutions to any problem.'
Tell your child there is always a way of resolving any kind of problem.

▶ **Do it every time your child comes to you with a problem before you start exploring the problem.**

e.g. 'I fell out with Anna today. She doesn't want to be my friend anymore!' After empathising, tell them: 'What do we know about problems? That we can always sort them out. Let's find a solution. Let's start by…'

▼ 83%

4 mins

Let Them Face the Consequences

> When you have to choose a single option from an apparently limitless range of possibilities, you're curbing the Need For Autonomy. This is why decision-making is so hard.

❯ Before agreeing to the decision your child just made, check that they understand its consequences. Tell them firmly that they won't be able to go back on their choice.

Think of 3 situations in which your child changed their mind and you didn't take a firm stance.

How could you have told them WHAT they needed to do so that they took responsibility for their choices?

▼ 85%

Episode 33

🕐 6 mins

Techniques You Already Know

Technique 1: Asking their opinion

▶ Give 3 examples of questions that you could ASK your child when you WANT TO KNOW their opinion about something.

_____

_____

_____

_____

Technique 2: Making your thoughts visible

▶ Draw a short diagram of the decision-making process that you have gone through. Set aside some time today to show it to your child.

_____

_____

_____

_____

Technique 3: Letting natural consequences occur
Leave your child time to play by themselves.
Remember this technique when making decisions about your child's scheduled activities.

Technique 4: Implementing a family decision-making process
Every time you have to make a decision, go through the whole process you learnt in this chapter and teach it to your child too.

▼ 87%

Score: /12

What Have You Learnt so Far?

Congratulations!
You've completed **Chapter 6**.

Take this self-evaluation test to see how well you've taken on board the information we've shared with you. Depending on the results, you'll see whether what you've learnt has sunk in or whether you need to watch some episodes again. Check your answers at the end of the Playbook.

 If you'd like to know your result immediately without having to add up scores, you can take the test **online.** Go to **bit.ly/TestChapter6** or scan the QR code.

1. From the list below, choose the 6 skills that are important for developing into a happy future adult.

- **a.** Self-discipline
- **b.** Knowing how to manipulate
- **c.** The ability to say no
- **d.** Handling emotions
- **e.** Controlling impulses
- **f.** The power to only do what you want
- **g.** Social skills
- **h.** Self-Esteem
- **i.** The ability to overcome adversity
- **j.** The knowledge to make decisions and solve problems

90% ▼

2. **How does the knowledge to make decisions and solve problems come about?**

a. It develops over time. An older child will have a more developed sense of this skill.

b. It develops from age 5, around the age children start school.

c. It takes practice. Help your child to develop this ability from a young age.

3. **Your child is angry. Their classmates have been laughing at them because they spilled water on their top. How do you react?**

a. You don't really have time to listen to their stories. They always come to you at the worst possible moment.

b. Put what you are doing aside or ask them to give you a few minutes to finish the urgent work that you are doing, after which you will listen to the whole story, however long it takes.

c. It takes too long for them to explain. It apparently started in PE but now we're onto lunchtime. You can't make head nor tail of it. You try to be patient, but after a while you give up.

4. **Your child was told off by the history teacher and given detention. How do you react?**

a. 'What did you do?! Why are teachers telling you off? Didn't I tell you to watch your mouth? That's all we need. You'd better buck up your ideas.'

b. 'You're going to have to go to your next class early and apologise. I also want you to turn in some extra homework.'

c. 'What happened? I'm sure you felt bad when she picked you to answer the question. Imagine how your teacher felt when you...'

92% ▼

5. You gave money to your child for a trip, but they lost it before they could give it to the teacher. How do you react?

a. Empathise with your child's feelings. They already feel bad enough about losing the money. Then try to run through the circumstances in which the money was lost and find a solution together.

b. 'But of course you lost it. Can't you take care of anything?'

c. 'You're not going on any more trips. If you can't look after money, then you'll stay at home!'

6. Your daughter is crying because her boyfriend has dumped her. How do you react?

a. 'Come on, dry your eyes. He's not going to want you back looking like that.'

b. 'That's the least of your problems! There will be plenty of time for boys when you're older! You're better off without him. At least now you can take your homework seriously.'

c. 'I imagine that you're feeling pretty sad about what happened, aren't you? Tell me all about it.'

7. Which of the following are the child's responsibility and therefore generically called 'children's problems'?

a. Dealing with the consequences of their actions, pocket money, handling emotions of those around them, relationships with other children.

b. Following the rules, seeing tasks through to the end, relationships with the adults in their life.

c. Children shouldn't have problems. It is the responsibility of parents to keep them away from any worries or concerns that may affect them in the long term.

d. Relationships with other children, school and related activities, handling their own emotions, other problems related to childhood responsibilities.

95% ▼

8. Which of the following are the parent's responsibility (hence we use the generic term 'adult's problems'?)

a. Their own or other people's property, beliefs, principles and societal norms, health and safety, education and household rules.

b. Everything that a child is not able to deal with themselves.

c. Until the child is old enough, absolutely all problems should be solved by parents. You cannot leave a child to solve problems they don't know how to handle, as it would damage their Self-Esteem.

d. Even when they're small, by trial and error, a child should be able to learn how to handle their problems by themselves. Parents should only intervene in emergencies.

9. The rules that you set in your house and in the relationship you have with your child are your problem.

a. True

b. False

10. At what age do parents cease to make decisions about 'adult's problems'?

a. 14

b. When their child has developed the necessary awareness in each of these categories.

c. 18, when they're legally responsible for themselves. Until then, parents have to make decisions.

97% ▼

11. In what order do you tackle a problem?

a. 1. Sentiments — tell them not to cry, since it's not that bad.
2. Solutions — you tell them to grow up and sort it out themselves.
3. Success — they try out different options. In the end, they'll learn how to solve problems.

b. 1. Sentiments — first of all, let out all those emotions.
2. Situation — look at the situation from all angles.
3. Solutions — ask questions. Your child will find the solution for themselves or you can help them.
4. Success — see the plan through and make sure they follow it. Give them feedback about their approach and the results.

c. 1. Situation — look at what actually happened
2. Solutions — explain to your child what needs doing to make things right.
3. Sentiments — encourage them to say that everything is going to be OK.
4. Success — your child will believe in themselves and will solve their problem.

12. How do you react when your child goes back on a decision?

a. Don't give them either option, so that they learn the consequences and won't keep changing their mind.

b. Give them the second option. At the end of the day, they made a choice.

c. Teach them the consequences of their choices. Take a firm stance and don't offer them the second option.

100% ▼

Jot down any other ideas or notes you want to remember from this chapter here.

Notes

Chapter 6: Solving Problems and Making Decisions

PARENTING PLAYBOOK

APPENDIX

Appendix

The Answers to the Exercises and Tests

How to use the Appendix

In the appendix, you will find worksheets with exercises that you can use and do over and over again.

Every time you see this symbol , it means that you will find the same exercise in the appendix.

To get the most out of these worksheets, you can photocopy them or download them from

https://uk.allaboutparenting.com/appendix/

Fill them in every time a situation demands it, for each of your children (if you have more than one) or after a period to see your progress.

How to Set Rules and Boundaries

Rules about bedtime and waking up

Rules about eating

The Parenting Playbook Appendix

Rules about hygiene

Rules for a peaceful home

Rules about screens

Rules about personal property

Your Child's Performance

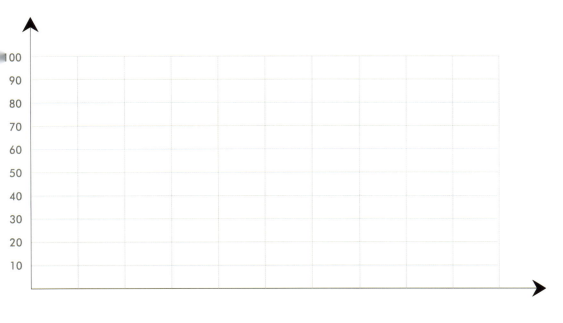

Your Child's Responsibilities

Day:

What they have to do:

Day:

What they have to do:

Day:

What they have to do:

Day:

What they have to do:

Day:

What they have to do:

Day:

What they have to do:

Our Expectations For

Relating to: ....

Daily	Weekly	Monthly

Relating to: ....

Daily	Weekly	Monthly

How to Set Rules and Boundaries

War zones	Rule: What do you expect to happen?	When?	How?

Under what conditions?	Exceptions	Consequences for breaking the rules

Weekly Schedule

Monday

Tuesday

Wednesday

Thursday

Friday

Saturday

Sunday

The Parenting Playbook Appendix

Routine for

Draw the steps with your child

1.

2.

3.

4.

1. _____
2. _____
3. _____
4. _____

Planning Ahead

Scenario:

_____

_____

What do you expect to happen?

_____

_____

_____

_____

What does your family expect of you?

_____

_____

_____

_____

_____

_____

Your Child's Abilities

Strenghts

Areas for improvement

Abilities to develop

Solving Problems

Bringing SENTIMENTS
to the surface

Exploring the SITUATION

Finding SOLUTIONS

Measuring SUCCESS

Making Decisions

1. Objective

2. Criteria

Criteria NEEDS	Criteria WANTS

3. Alternatives

4. Compare the alternatives by their criteria. Write down your decision.

Answers

Chapter 1

Episode 11: 1. Natural and Logical 2. Safe and Immediate

Episode 12: 1. That we're stimulating learning, not causing suffering. 2. If you choose a type of behaviour, you also choose its consequences.

Test

1. b 2. c 3. b 4. b 5. a 6. b 7. c 8. a 9. b 10. c

Chapter 2

Episodes 8 and 9: My child does not belong to me; I love my child unconditionally; I can't force someone to change their behaviour; Behaviour is a choice; Mistakes are learning opportunities; Parents are role models for their children; Behaviour is a choice; The way they refer to household activities and decisions; Parents focus on the unique ability of their child; Educate yourself so you can educate your child.

Episode 16: Relatedness; Competence; Autonomy.

Episode 27: 1. In the need to trust and feel safe with the adults that care for them. They seek to satisfy this need by crying. 2. The Need for Competence and the Need for Autonomy.

Episode 28: 1. The Need for Competence; 2. Give them control over certain things they want to do, but within your limits.

Test

1.a,b,c 2.b 3.a,b,c,f 4.b,c,d,e,f 5.a,b,d,e,f 6.d 7.c 8.c 9.b 10.c

Chapter 3

Episode 4: 1. a. T b. F c. T 2. b. Image-Esteem 3. b. From being excessively praised.

Episode 5: 1.a. With fear. b. 'It's not my fault I didn't succeed. Things were against me'. c. Won't ask for what's rightfully theirs.

d. Settles for 'good enough'.

2. Things that you can't control.

Episode 7: **1.** The Need for Relatedness manifests itself as the feeling of being loved just as you are; the Need for Competence manifests itself as the feeling of being able to face challenges; the Need for Autonomy manifests itself as the feeling of having control over your own existence. When I feel compelled to do something I don't want to, I find sources of motivation in the outcome, convictions, principles and looking for the positive.

2. 1. 'I love myself as I am' 2. 'I deserve it. I have a right to a happy life.' **3.** 'I have choices and decisions to make.' **4.** 'I feel competent. I feel that I'm good at what I'm doing.'

Episode 8: **1.** c. They feel inadequate, unloved and like they're in the way. 2. c. From 8 months.

Episode 9: **1.** 'I know that you're a generous person...'; 'We don't hit in this family.'

2. 'He's not shy. He'll speak when he feels the need to.' 'She is beautiful. All children are beautiful. You know, she's really friendly too?' 'What he did wasn't very nice, was it? How will you react next time?'

Episode 10: 1. Focuses on Image-Esteem; Encourages an acceptance of negative behaviour from others so as to be like everyone else; Instils the conviction that 'I'm not good enough'; Can't accept themselves as they are; Feels inadequate and like they're not good enough; Continually comparing themselves to others.

2. 'It's cold. It's not the right temperature for just a T-shirt.' 'You know, everyone has come to the restaurant to have a nice time. We care about how other people feel around us. The way you're behaving might bother other people, so I'm asking you to stay in your seat and to speak in a calmer tone.'

Episode 11: 1. Bullying; the expression 'You're making a fool of yourself'; Children hauled in front of the class to be made fun of.
2. b. If I don't do what mum says, I could be abandoned at any time.
3. a. I have to change to be worthy of love; b. If my parents don't love me as I am, nobody will.
4. a, b, c.

Episode 12: c. 'I love you, whatever you decide.'; d. 'The most important thing for me is that you are happy with your own choices.' f. Showing love is healthy; i. Unconditional love is when you feel loved in all circumstances...

Episode 14: b. It's not right that I'm sitting here.

Episode 20: It's part of their personality. That's how they choose to express themselves. Self-Esteem is likely to increase. Any penchant for an outlandish dress style won't last long.

Episode 21: 1. Image-Esteem / Self-Esteem 2. Suboptimal 3. Affirmation

Episode 22:
Unhealthy competition: a, c, h, i, j.
Healthy competition: b, d, e, f, g.

Episode 23: 1. Player: equal; Rules: followed; Results: might win, might lose; **2.** a.

Test
1. Self-Esteem: a, c, d, f; **Image-Esteem** b, e, g, h.
2. a, c, e, f; **3.** a, g, h.
4. Expressions to avoid: 'Why can't you just be a good student, like your sister?'; 'Wow, so clever!'— In a sarcastic way; 'Naughty child!'; 'That's how he is, he's shy.'; 'Can you see any other children running around the restaurant?'; 'What grades did everyone else get?'; 'I'm ashamed of you!'; 'If you don't come with me now, I'm

going to leave you here!'

Expressions to keep: 'I love you just the way you are.'; 'I know you're a good boy.'; 'I believe in you. You can sort this argument out with your words.'; 'You didn't behave very well just then.'; 'I love you no matter what you do.'; 'I like being with you.'; 'I love you both equally, but in different ways, because you're different.'; 'Every person is unique.'

5.b **6.**b **7.**c **8.**a **9.**c **10.**c

Chapter 4

Episode 5: Authoritarian Parent: c, f, h; Permissive Parent: a, e; Balanced Parent: b, d, g.

Episode 16: 'yet'.

Episode 18: 1. If you only concentrate on the negatives, motivation will decrease; 2. Your child will lose the motivation to learn and do those specific activities; 3. The child will become a critical and self-critical person.

Test

1. b **2.** b,d,h,g,f; **3.**1.A 2.E 3.P 4.E 5.A 6.E 7.A 8.A 9.E.
4. I have the theoretical knowledge — I know; Skills — I practice and have experience — I can; Results in Optimal Motivation — I want.
5.c; **6.**a; **7.** c; **8.**c; **9.**c; **10.**b.

Chapter 5

Episodes 3-4: 1. Bribe; 2. Threat; 3. Negotiation; 4. False promises; 5. Force; 6. 'You are not allowed to'; 7. Giving in.

Episode 5: 1. To have your child's cooperation, to have optimal motivation; 2. To use these techniques to fulfil all 3 Basic Psychological Needs.

Episode 6: 1. You want somebody to change their behaviour, but they don't want to; 2. Somebody is insisting that you change your behaviour, but you don't want to; 3. 2 people in a relationship, each suggesting things neither of them wants to do; 4. You put yourself forward to do something that you don't actually want to do.

Test

1.b 2.b, d, f 3.a 4.c 5.a 6.c 7. c 8.c, f 9.b 10.c 11. c 12.c.

Chapter 6

Episode 12: 1. Is there a difference between the expectation and the current situation?; 2. Is the cause unknown?; 3. Do you need to know the cause to solve the problem or reduce its effects?
Problem refers to the past, decision refers to the future.

Episode 14: 1. We focus on our child's sentiments and empathise with the messages they're sending; 2. We help our child express what they want to say and come to a diagnosis; 3. We find a solution; 4. We measure how successful we were in implementing these solutions.

Test

1.a, d, e, g, h, j. 2.c. 3.b. 4.c. 5.a. 6.c. 7.d. 8.a. 9.a. 10.b. 11.b. 12.c.